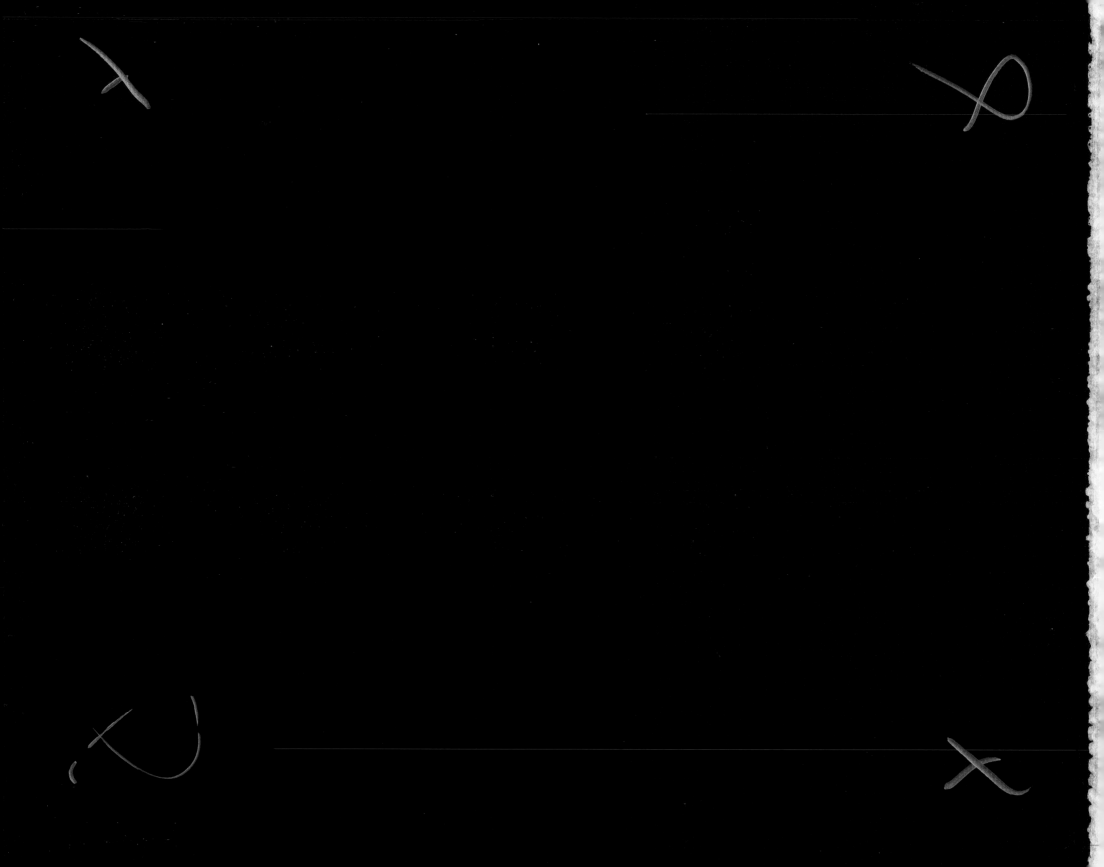

Transforming the World

Rochester at 150

Transforming the World

Rochester at 150

STEVEN J. KEILLOR

cherbo publishing group, inc.

president	JACK C. CHERBO
chief operating officer	ELAINE HOFFMAN
editorial director	CHRISTINA M. BEAUSANG
managing feature editor	MARGARET L. MARTIN
feature editor	ERICA RHEINSCHILD
senior profiles editor	J. KELLEY YOUNGER
profiles editors	BENJAMIN PROST
	LIZA YETENEKIAN SMITH
associate editor	SYLVIA EMRICH-TOMA
editorial assistants/proofreaders	JENNY KORNFELD
	REBECCA SAUER
profiles writers	B. D. CAMPBELL
	SYLVIA EMRICH-TOMA
	TERRI JONISCH
	JO ELLEN KRUMM
creative director	PERI A. HOLGUIN
senior designer	THEODORE E. YEAGER
designer	NELSON CAMPOS
senior photo editor	WALTER MLADINA
photo editors	ANDREA GREEN
	KAREN MAZE
digital color specialist	ART VASQUEZ
sales administrator	JOAN K. BAKER
client services supervisor	PATRICIA DE LEONARD
senior client services coordinator	LESLIE E. SHAW
client services coordinator	KENYA HICKS
executive assistant	JUDY ROBITSCHEK
administrative assistant	BILL WAY
regional sales manager	RICHARD R. FRY

Cherbo Publishing Group, Inc.
Encino, California 91316
© 2007 by Cherbo Publishing Group, Inc.
All rights reserved. Published 2007.

Printed in Canada
By Friesens

Subsidiary Production Office
Santa Rosa, CA, USA
888.340.6049

Library of Congress Cataloging-in-Publication data
Keillor, Steven J.
A pictorial guide highlighting Rochester's
economic, political, and social history.
Library of Congress Control Number: 2007933303
ISBN 978-1-882933-81-5

Visit the CPG Web site at www.cherbopub.com.

Peace Plaza

Acknowledgments

My appreciative thanks go to the staff of the Rochester Public Library, the Minnesota Historical Society reference library at the History Center in St. Paul, and the Olmsted County Historical Society. Bob and Eunice Davis, of New Haven township, have graciously given me a place to stay during my research trips to Rochester. Thanks to Erica Rheinschild of Cherbo Publishing Group for wisely guiding this manuscript through the editing process, and to Margaret Martin of Cherbo Publishing Group for inviting me to participate in this publication.

Silver Lake

Pedestrian subway

COMPANIES & ORGANIZATIONS PROFILED

The following companies and organizations have made a valuable commitment to the quality of this publication. The City of Rochester gratefully acknowledges their participation in *Transforming the World: Rochester at 150*.

International Brotherhood of Electrical Workers Local 343
9 80th Street SE, Rochester, MN 55904
Phone: 507-282-7081 / Fax: 507-282-1562
Contact: Al Stork, Business Manager
E-mail: al@ibewlocal343.org
Web site: www.ibewlocal343.org

An Oshkosh Truck Corporation Company

McNeilus Truck and Manufacturing, Inc.
524 County Road 34 East, Dodge Center, MN 55927
Phone: 507-374-8248 / Fax: 507-374-6394
Contact: Jeffry Swertfeger, Director,
Marketing and Communications
E-mail: jswert@mcneilusco.com
Web site: www.mcneiluscompanies.com

Kahler Hotel Properties
20 Second Avenue SW, Rochester, MN 55902
Phone: 507-280-6200 / Fax: 507-285-2701
Web site: www.kahler.com

Rochester Public Utilities
4000 East River Road, Rochester, MN 55906
Phone: 507-280-1534 / Fax: 507-280-1542
Contact: Tony Benson, Communications Coordinator
E-mail: tbenson@rpu.org
Web site: www.rpu.org

Mayo Clinic
200 First Street SW, Rochester, MN 55905
Phone: 507-284-2511 / Fax: 507-284-0161
Web site: www.mayoclinic.org/rochester

Rochester Marriott Mayo Clinic Area

Prescotts

From left: T. Denny Sanford Pediatric Center at the Mayo Clinic; 2007 Rochesterfest; 7th Street and 5th Avenue Southeast

Welcome. We are building an inclusive community.

It is a privilege and an honor to welcome you on behalf of the City of Rochester to *Transforming the World: Rochester at 150*. As you turn the pages, you will see that Rochester is an exciting, diverse, and growing city with a rich history. This history is based on hospitality and service, founded on the contributions of the Mayo Clinic.

While the service industry is our roots, the technology industry has also flourished in Rochester. IBM and other large and small businesses have become integral components in Rochester's success. Designated as an All-American City and a Star City, Rochester has been consistently recognized as one of the best places to live in America.

Rochester has placed a strong emphasis on K–12 education and is committed to higher education, notably Rochester Community and Technical College, Winona State University, and the new, increased presence of the University of Minnesota Rochester.

I am especially pleased with our dedication to art and culture. From the expanded and dynamic Peace Plaza to numerous festivals—Rochesterfest, WinterFest, and ARTStoberFEST—and from the Rochester Art Center to the Rochester Civic Theatre and Down by the Riverside concerts, art and culture are adding to the vibrancy of the city.

As we celebrate the 150th anniversary of our founding, August 5, 1858, I hope you share the pride I have in this great city of 100,000 citizens.

Ardell F. Brede

Mayor Ardell F. Brede
Rochester, Minnesota

FOREWORD

When I graduated from Rochester High School in 1946, I told my parents I was going to leave "this hick town forever." Like most 17-year-olds, I thought I knew everything. Off I went to Amherst College, then Yale Law School, then to Korea with the U.S. Marines. By 1955, after seeing "the world," I was delighted to come back to Rochester with my bride, and I've never wanted to leave again.

I ended up working for Harry Blackmun, who at the time was legal counsel to the Mayo Clinic. During the late 1950s, Mayo had approximately 3,000 employees. Today, in Rochester, they employ over 30,000.

Rochester has grown right alongside Mayo. When I left town in 1946, there were 27,000 residents. We have 100,000 today, and our numbers keep growing each year. Just as Mayo attracts patients and visitors from all over the world, our low unemployment rate draws a diverse labor force.

And Rochester has room to grow. Our suburbs are expanding, while exciting developments are adding to our downtown's allure. The latter includes not only residential properties but also the new Minnesota BioBusiness Center, the result of a partnership between the Mayo Clinic and the University of Minnesota to finance and support genomics research. The University of Minnesota will also open a new facility downtown with 55,000 square feet of classroom space primarily for scientific and technological higher education courses.

But it is not just medicine and business that brings people to Rochester. Rochester offers a variety of lifestyles from rural to suburban to urban. Our fine quality of life, our excellent schools and health care, our exciting cultural attractions, and our diverse and growing economy make for a great place to live, work, and raise a family.

Come to Rochester. You'll never want to leave.

A. M. "Sandy" Keith

A. M. "Sandy" Keith
Executive Director
Rochester Downtown Alliance

Born and raised in Rochester, Mr. Keith served as state senator (1959–1963), lieutenant governor (1963–1967), associate justice of the Minnesota Supreme Court (1989–1990), and chief justice (1990–1998).

ROCHESTER TIMELINE

1854   1883   1907

Winona & St. Peter Railroad, circa 1865

1854 Edward Slade Smith and a group of speculators stake a claim on land that will later become downtown Rochester.

1854 George and Jonathan Head purchase Smith's site for $3,600. George Head settles the area and names it after Rochester, New York.

1858 Rochester is incorporated as a city.

Charles H. Mayo (left), William W. Mayo (center), and William J. Mayo (right), circa 1900

Henry Plummer, circa 1936

1864 The Winona & St. Peter Railroad is the first train to arrive in Rochester.

Damage from the 1883 tornado

1883 On August 21st, a tornado devastates Rochester, destroying more than 150 buildings, killing 26 people, and injuring more than 100 others.

1889 The Sisters of St. Francis build Saint Marys Hospital in Rochester to accommodate the growing medical practice of Dr. William W. Mayo, one of the first specialists in surgery. His sons, William J. and Charles H. Mayo, will eventually take over the practice and bring it to international prominence.

1907 Dr. Henry Plummer of the Mayo Clinic designs the first system of comprehensive medical records in which each patient is assigned a single file containing all hospital records. Previously, hospital departments maintained separate files on patients.

1938 The Mayo Civic Auditorium, later known as the Mayo Civic Center, opens. Its two large venues, a sports arena and a fine arts theater, will create a new cultural and enter-tainment center in Rochester.

1947 Renowned architect Frank Lloyd Wright designs a house built of cement block and cypress wood for Dr. A. H. Bulbulian. Within 10 years, Wright will design two more homes in Rochester: the Thomas E. Keys house and the James B. McBean house.

Rochester Junior College, circa 1925

1934 President Franklin D. Roosevelt attends a ceremony in Rochester honoring Drs. Charles H. and William J. Mayo for their service to disabled war veterans, whom they treated free of charge.

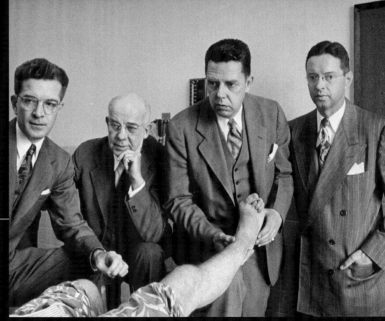

Edward C. Kendall (second from left) and Philip S. Hench (third from left) at the Mayo Clinic, 1948

1915 Classes begin at Minnesota's first community college, Rochester Junior College. The college will be renamed Rochester Community and Technical College in 1996.

President Franklin D. Roosevelt in Rochester, 1934

1950 Drs. Edward C. Kendall and Philip S. Hench of the Mayo Clinic win the Nobel Prize in Physiology and Medicine for the discovery of cortisone and its use in treating rheumatoid arthritis.

ROCHESTER TIMELINE

1952   1961   1969   1980

1952 Miracle Mile, the first large shopping center in Minnesota outside of the Twin Cities, opens in Rochester.

1953 Rochester's first television station, KROC TV, later known as KTTC TV, goes on the air.

1958 IBM dedicates a 570,000-square-foot plant in Rochester to produce data processing machines. The site's workforce will grow to a peak of 8,100 in 1990–91.

Lea Thompson, 2006

1961 Actress Lea Thompson is born in Rochester. She will go on to star in the *Back to the Future* film trilogy and the television series *Caroline in the City*.

1969 Dr. Mark Coventry, a Mayo Clinic surgeon, performs the first total hip replacement surgery approved by the Food and Drug Administration.

1973 The Mayo Clinic is the first medical institution in the country—and the second in the world—to install a computed tomography (CT) scanner.

1978 Heavy rains begin on July 5th. The storm runoff raises the Zumbro River to a record 23 feet, producing a major flood that causes $40 million in damages.

Eric Strobel (number 19) and the U.S. hockey team at the winter Olympics, 198[0]

1980 In a surprise victory over the Soviet Olympic hockey team, Rochester native Eric Strobel and the rest of the "Miracle on Ice" U.S. hockey team win the gold medal at the winter Olympics in Lake Placid, New York.

Construction of IBM's Rochester plant, circa 1956

1983   1993   1995   2001

1983 The first Rochesterfest is held. The annual summer celebration will draw crowds with musical performances, hot-air balloons, food, a parade, a lumberjack contest, and more.

Soldiers Field Veterans Memorial

2001 Shjon Podein, a Rochester native, wins the Stanley Cup playing for the Colorado Avalanche National Hockey League team.

2006 Somerby Golf Club in Byron, near Rochester, hosts the Showdown at Somerby, a PGA Nationwide Tour event. The club will also host the Showdown in 2007.

Shjon Podein with the National Hockey League's King Clancy Memorial Trophy, 2001

Rochesterfest, 1990

1993 *Money* magazine names Rochester the best place to live in America. Rochester will top *Money*'s list of "America's Best Small Cities" in 1999.

1995 The Zumbro River Flood Control Project is completed. With an estimated cost of $106 million, the project includes new levees and reservoirs to help protect the city against future floods.

2000 The Soldiers Field Veterans Memorial is dedicated in Rochester. Honoring veterans from southeast Minnesota, the memorial features granite walls with engraved war scenes and the names of veterans who died in service.

Somerby Golf Club

PART ONE

THE RISE TO PROMINENCE

A History of Rochester

Rochester, 1868

CHAPTER ONE

The Place on the Land

It began with the land, at a place where eastern woods met western prairies. No clear line of truce separated them, but an intermittent warfare persisted, as prairie fires advanced east one year, then oaks and aspens spread their young growth west again, until a year when the flames returned. Small outposts of brush or saplings survived even then, here and there. The nearly 30 inches of rain that fell on good loam soil each year could sustain forest if the fires permitted. Watering prairie grass or young oak trees with an indifferent neutrality was a network of spring-fed brooks, small creeks, and the south fork of a river that flowed north and east to the Mississippi River. More or less permanent stands of oaks and aspens grew on bottomlands where stream waters halted the flames.

Zumbro River

The last glaciers had not advanced this far east, so there were no lakes. Yet the melting at the glaciers' edge 40 miles west had drained through this area and created a dense network of streams. The sheer volume of water enabled the main stream, the south fork, to carve out a valley more than 200 feet deep in places, through the underlying limestone and sandstone. Spring-fed brooks also fed the south fork.

This land and its waters were visited by prehistoric peoples of the Eastern Archaic and Woodland cultures—nomadic hunters and gatherers who had to use every available niche to find enough food to survive. Visits here increased as the Woodland people began to use bows and arrows for deer hunts in the fall and winter. Yet greater resources beckoned in the rich, wide floodplain of the Great River 50 miles east. Centered at Cahokia, near present-day East St. Louis, Illinois, a Mississippian culture of settled villages raising corn came north around AD 1100, depopulating interior valleys like the south fork by offering a more dependable diet on terraces above the Mississippi's bottomlands.

Around that time, a people calling themselves Dakota, or "allies," migrated from the Ohio River valley to the mouth of the Minnesota River and north of there. More nomadic and less agricultural than Mississippians, they hunted game, harvested wild rice, and warred with surrounding Indian nations. Encountering the Dakota in the late 17th century, the French brought them into the historic era of written accounts and numbered centuries. Rival Ojibwe forced two Dakota tribes—the Mdewakanton and Wahpekute—to move south into the Mississippi valley by 1800. Mdewakanton Chief Red Wing's band lived just north of Lake Pepin, and Chief Wapahasha's band lived south of it. A Wahpekute village lay some 60 miles up the Cannon River from Red Wing's band. The Dakota had no village at the south fork, and its waterfall was of no real use to them.

They called this river Wazi Oju, "the place of the pine tree." A few majestic white pines grew on islands and on the riverbanks. Returning Dakota hunters likely used them as landmarks when returning to Red Wing's or Wapahasha's villages.

Wapahasha controlled hunting lands along the Wazi Oju. Eager for navigable streams for their fur trade, the French called it Les Embarras, meaning "the obstructions," named for the driftwood and logs that blocked the lower river and kept it from being the trade route they desired.

The Dakota followed the seasons. Near summer villages of bark lodges along the Mississippi, they planted corn in May and spent the summer in small groups combing the countryside for game, berries, and edible plants until the corn harvest in September. Then they packed their tipis to head for the interior woods, which sheltered them from winter's winds while they hunted deer and small game until January. Every three years or so, they likely hunted near the Wazi Oju. By mid March they were hunting muskrats and collecting maple sugar. Then it was back to the bark lodges, and the cycle began anew.

This area on the margins of prairie and woodland was marginal to them. Vast prairies to the west offered them vast herds of buffalo. Thick forests to the east supported larger populations of deer, bear, and other game. Lakes to the north provided wild rice. They pursued what roamed the land or picked what grew wild on it and were uninterested in this area's waterfalls or its soil.

By 1800 French and British fur traders induced the Dakota to become commercial hunters and trappers, taking deerskins, beaver pelts, muskrat furs, and buffalo hides by the thousands in exchange for firearms, cloth, and other trade goods. As commercial hunters, the Dakota likely depleted the fur-bearing game along the Wazi Oju.

The United States acquired the lands west of the Mississippi from France in the Louisiana Purchase of 1803. By 1824 the U.S. Army had built Fort Snelling 80 miles north of the south fork, at the spot where the Minnesota River joined the Mississippi. The pace of change quickened on the Mississippi as steamboats and rafts of logs brought commerce and tourism. But the pace hardly quickened along the obstructed tributary 50 miles west. Taking a straight line across the prairie was faster than canoeing Les Embarras.

The Mdewakanton and Wahpekute sold their lands to the United States in August 1851. Change came to the interior. The government prepared to sell land to pioneers who would not be passing through but settling down to farm. The shifting battle lines of prairie and woods made little difference to pioneers who planned to turn it all into farmland. The lines that mattered were section, township, and county lines.

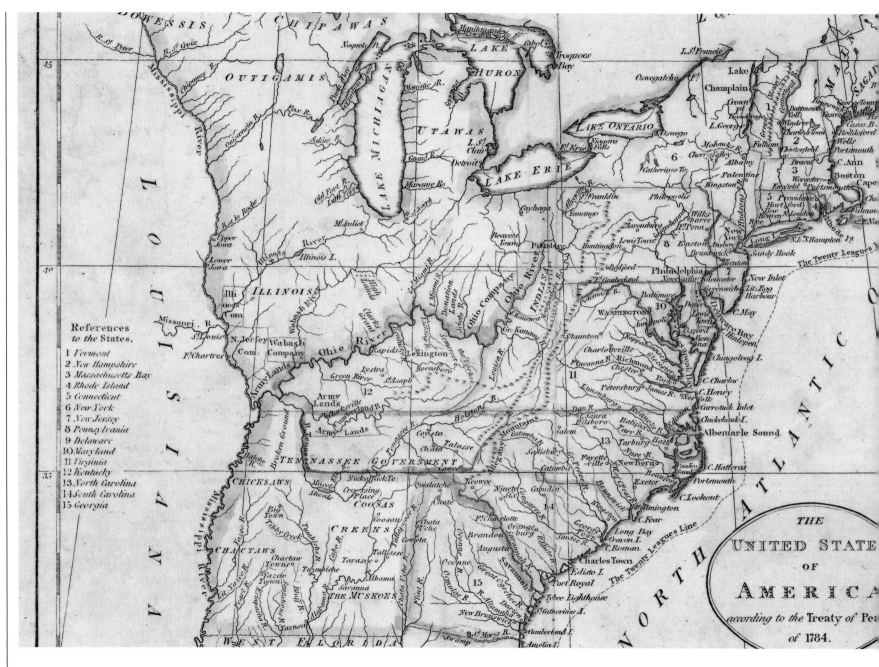

This page: Map of the United States, 1784. Opposite page, top: Northwest Ordinance, 1787. Opposite page, bottom: John Ball, circa 1862.

References to the States.
1 Vermont
2 New Hampshire
3 Massachusetts Bay
4 Rhode Island
5 Connecticut
6 New York
7 New Jersey
8 Pennsylvania
9 Delaware
10 Maryland
11 Virginia
12 Kentucky
13 North Carolina
14 South Carolina
15 Georgia

THE
UNITED STATES
OF
AMERICA
according to the Treaty of Peace
of 1784.

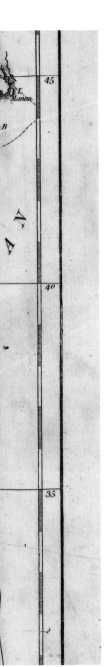

The Northwest Ordinance (1787) designed a plan whereby a new state like Minnesota could be built from the ground up. The plan would be etched right on the land, surveyed in a checker-board grid. Squares, measured as one-square-mile sections and 36-square-mile townships, would delineate land clearly to avoid title disputes. The squares would also be building blocks for a government—each parcel of land would support a voting citizen and his family. Township governments would be the building blocks for county governments, and the many counties would make the state itself.

Land would be sliced and diced into precise portions. Each family would settle on one portion and cooperate to maintain the schools, churches, and local governments needed to build a state. Ideally, each parcel had its family so that a scattering might not delay progress. This system, unlike the migratory Dakota and waterborne fur trade, would not leave the interior along the south fork unchanged.

Between September and October 1853, John Ball, a Winona surveyor, marked out the township boundaries along the south fork—Township 107 North, Range 14 West (later, Cascade township) and Township 106 North, Range 14 West (later, Rochester township). Both were in the 14th column of townships west of a line of longitude, the fifth principal meridian, running through eastern Arkansas and Missouri. One was the 107th township north of a line of latitude, or base line, also running through Arkansas, and the other was next in the row, or the 106th. The following summer, two other surveyors marked out the section lines within each township.

The U.S. government was the retailer set to sell these parcels, and it wanted surveyors to do more than measure out the merchandise. It hoped to make a profit as well as to encourage settlement. Surveyors were to note features, especially attractive ones that might commend a parcel to a purchaser. Other than gold, few features were more appealing than waterfalls, which could provide waterpower for mills and a site for a town. Along what surveyors called "the South fork of Embarrass River," they noted "a good mill site" with "falls 6 ft." and a "rock bottom & sides" that made a stable foundation for a mill. The river varied from 50 to 66 feet across, with a "gravelly bottom" and a "swift current."

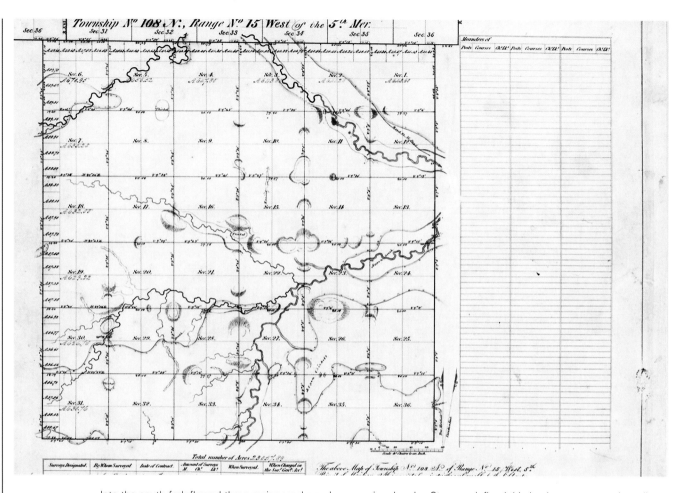

Into the south fork flowed three major creeks and some minor brooks. Streams defined this landscape, cut out its valleys, exposed its limestone and sandstone bluffs, deposited its floodplain soil, and sustained thin ribbons of mature trees below the higher ground covered with prairie grass and clumps of brush. Meandering bottomlands, oak groves, sloughs, and prairies did not geometrically match the grid pattern imposed upon this landscape. On the northernmost creek, near where it emptied into the river, was "a set of falls, the water falling some 10 ft." Pioneers named it Cascade Creek. That made two mill sites within 1.25 miles of each other.

Theoretically, surveyors were to precede pioneers and establish a legal framework on the ground. It often did not work out as planned. Here the surveyors found a road meandering from northwest to southeast through the two townships. A pioneer

This page: Olmsted County survey map, 1855. Opposite page, top: Early pioneers, circa 1880. Opposite page, bottom: Zumbro River.

16

stage line owner, M. O. Walker, of Chicago, was set to begin stagecoach service from Dubuque, Iowa, to St. Paul along this road—mainly to deliver mail in the winter when the Mississippi River route was frozen shut. This Dubuque Trail passed the mill site on the south fork, crossed a ford, and went close to the falls on Cascade Creek.

Also preceding the section-line surveyors was a party of men from Winona seeking promising town sites. Most land buyers planned to grow crops on the land, but some hoped the land itself would be their "crop"—its value increasing year by year until they harvested it with a hugely profitable sale. Such speculators could partly determine the size of the land's "harvest"—the number of lots per acre—by filing a plat at

the county courthouse, which divided a 640-acre section into perhaps 60 city blocks, each with 20 or so lots. That gave the town-site promoter 1,200 parcels to sell where the government had only offered four, eight, or 16 parcels. If the public believed in the town site's future, the lots would sell at ever-increasing prices.

Surveyor John Ball may have told the Winona men about the south fork, or perhaps it was Thomas Simpson, a Winona surveyor and leader. Edward Slade Smith led the group, heard a waterfall, and made a claim at the site. They were uninterested in settling on this land or in growing anything on it. They wanted to subdivide it to sell to others. After returning to Winona, the speculators hired a fellow to construct the log shanty needed to prove their right to the land.

FALLS IN ZUMBRO RIVER, NEAR ROCHESTER, MINN.

George and Jonathan Head landed there in mid July 1854 and started to demolish the hired house of Smith and his partners. Hearing of this intrusion, Smith returned before they could finish the job and confronted them with a drawn revolver. As an absentee claimant, Smith was at a disadvantage, for no county and no police existed there to enforce his claim. The Heads could simply return after he left. As a speculator, Smith sought a profit more than the land itself. He was satisfied when the Heads agreed to pay him $3,600 for the unimproved site, a hefty sum for vacant land, even if it did have a six-foot waterfall. Three days after the Heads bought the land, Walker's stagecoaches started to run past the mill site—a promising sign for the future.

The waterfall on Cascade Creek was not a contested site. Before the section surveyors arrived, the two claimants—Cummings and McReady—staked their claims, built their cabins, and jointly celebrated Fourth of July with a wagon ride and a fishing excursion. This creek was only 13 feet across and provided about one-fourth the waterpower of the Heads' site.

The Heads were interested in the waterpower that could make their site a city. They pounded in stakes that indicated where blocks and lots would lie on the land. George Head chose the name Rochester, after the city at the falls of the Genesee River in upstate New York. Perhaps he had read an Englishman's published description of it as a "bustling place" where "everything . . . appeared to be in motion. The very streets seemed to be starting up of their own accord, ready-made," as if "a great boxful of new houses had been sent by steam from New York, and tumbled out on the half-cleared land." Head certainly desired that growth for his Rochester.

George Head had to make his own streets. Oxen dragged a tree trunk in a straight line to clear brush and create Broadway in its place. Head supervised the construction of a crude bridge across the south fork. English-speaking settlers had wrestled with saying Les Embarras, pronounced "*lay-zahm-bah-rah*," and renamed it the Zumbro River. Head built a second log structure, which became a tavern for travelers on the Dubuque Trail. By the end of the summer of 1854, Head's Rochester had the rudimentary makings of a town.

He faced competition from Cummings and McReady's site on Cascade Creek. For the 1855 Fourth of July, the two sites competed to put on the best celebration. Head roasted a sheep; McReady, a steer. Fifty people came to each—a tie. The people who came, the people on whom each site's future depended, were farmers. They were keenly interested in the prairie grasses and trees and the soil underneath.

Surveyors had noted several areas. On Head's land were scattered groves of mainly bur oak, short and scrubby, mixed with brush. To the south and west grew quaking and bigtooth aspen, oaks, elms, and basswood. To the west of Head and McReady's sites was brush prairie, where the prairie grass dominated except for even shorter and scrubbier isolated bur oak and aspen, and some shrubs or thickets of hazel, willow, wolfberry, and Juneberry. Fire kept the trees small, short, few, and far between.

Loam soil formed from the slow decay of leaves, grass, and other residue of this vegetation—and from loess, loam dust from the glacial drift to the west that the winds blew in and deposited. The latest glacier had not reached Rochester, so no boulders

were deposited there, and the wind had blown none in either. Farmers appreciated the lack of rock-gathering chores. Much of this land could quickly be plowed and planted with small grains, especially the frontier's chief cash-raising and mortgage-lifting crop, wheat.

Town site promoters, however, sought faster, greater returns than even the best soil could produce. They knew a railroad or county-seat status would raise land values almost overnight. In 1855 Rochester became the county seat of Olmsted County, and in 1857, the Minnesota territorial legislature approved a Transit Railroad running through Rochester. The future looked promising indeed.

CHAPTER TWO

Producing Goods to Ship by Rail

In December 1856, the *St. Paul Advertiser* reported that Rochester had "a fine flouring mill" on the Zumbro, "a steam saw mill, a half a dozen stores, four hotels, [and] a population of five or six hundred." In April 1857, the month the legislature decided on the Transit Railroad through Rochester, a visitor noted, "At Rochester we found all bustle and excitement, owing in part to the railroad news." Yet he was cautious. "They are asking prices for real estate far in advance of the times."

2

Rochester, 1868

J. D. BLAKE & CO.,

DRY GOODS, NOTIONS, CLOTHING,

GENTS' FURNISHING GOODS,

Hats, Caps, Furs, Carpetings, Oil Cloths, &c.,

—AND—

MERCHANT TAILORS,

Heaney's Block, Rochester, Minnesota.

That proved true. The Panic of 1857 hit the nation that September, causing real estate values to plummet and delaying for seven years the first train crossing the Zumbro. Like a hailstorm or cyclone destroying the wheat crop, the Panic devastated the town-lot "crop." Urban real estate was an uncertain crop after all. Rochester would have to depend on the slower crops that the land produced. It was well situated to do so—the surrounding land was suited for wheat, which could be ground into flour; waterfalls could power the grinding; and the Zumbro River and Cascade Creek had waterfalls. When a railroad arrived, it could transport the flour.

While awaiting the railroad, Rochester's businesses sold goods to farmers, although farmers' lack of a nearby cash market for all their wheat hindered the local economy. By March 1858, general stores, hardware stores, drugstores, and miscellaneous retail establishments advertised in local newspapers. The Rochester Brewery bought barley from farmers and gave them one source of cash. Chandler & Ayers Meat Market offered cash for livestock. Wilson & Taylor dry goods store insisted that customers pay cash but offered to buy lumber, oats, or flour "at market prices"—bartering oats for goods, really. Flour miller Frederick A. Olds ran a general store, which presumably meant farmers could barter their wheat for Olds's "Ready-Made Clothing" or "Yankee Notions."

That March the editor of the *Rochester Free Press* walked the business district to survey the stores. At Olds's store, he "found the door open but no one in"—which indicated small-town trust—and he looked around inside at "a fair supply of Dry Goods, Groceries, etc." David Lesuer's New York Cheap Cash Store undoubtedly did not offer goods on credit or through barter, to keep its prices cheap. The editor did not forget to praise his advertisers wherever he walked. He noted that Henry Cross "keeps good Groceries, good provisions, and withal is good looking himself." John R. Cook ran a dry goods and a hardware store. In his hardware department, a tinsmith manufactured tin pots and pans and finished off the locally made stoves.

Cook's tinsmith revealed one advantage of having no railroad yet: local craftsmen manufactured for this local market with no fear of distant, large-scale factories shipping in lower-priced, higher-quality goods by rail. The Rochester Cabinet Shop could make cupboards, tables, and other furniture; Olds could grind flour; and the brewers could brew ale with little fear of competition from outsiders.

Processed goods like flour or beer could be hauled by wagon to distant markets, while wheat or barley could not. Rochester was inland, 50 miles from the nearest river port, Winona, and the road there was a difficult, treacherous one. Some 44 miles east, at Stockton, the wagon road ascended a precipitous path up the bluff before descending to Winona. Costs of hauling might be paid in life and limb as well as in dollars and in days of travel.

On August 5, 1858, the state incorporated Rochester as a city, divided into three wards. The *Rochester Democrat* worried that Republicans at the north end would control city offices, but the mayor's job rotated among the leading businessmen as a civic duty and not as a springboard to higher political office.

Frederick Olds's $40,000 Rochester flour mill was Minnesota's largest according to the census of 1860. The city's mayor in 1860, Olds purchased 210,000 bushels of wheat and 90,000 bushels of corn from area farmers, ground 42,000 barrels of flour and 25,000 barrels of corn meal, employed six men, and produced $171,000 worth of meal and flour. He gave farmers a partial, local cash market for wheat. Olds's advertisement instructed them how to prepare and sow their wheat seed. To invest on this scale, he expected a railroad soon in Rochester. Local residents could not consume 40,000 barrels of flour, so he had to wait and export most of it.

PHOTOGRAPHED UNDER THE AUSPICES OF THE
WINONA AND SAINT PETER R. R. CO.

IN THE BLUFFS,
On the Winona and St. Peter Railroad.

The Transit Railroad did a preliminary survey in June 1857, but the Panic and the steep bluff west of Winona greatly delayed further progress. Not until December 1862 did the first train travel the first six miles to Stockton. By then it was the Winona & St. Peter Railroad (W&SP). The W&SP came to Rochester on October 12, 1864. "JUBILATE! JUBILATE!" exclaimed one writer. "We bid adieu to the Stockton Hills, and the weary and everlasting jostlings and joundings, and aches and pains . . . they have caused us." A depot and a grain elevator were built along the tracks west of Main Street.

By June 1866, an active trade in wheat brought 28,000 bushels to the elevator in three days. During the Civil War, wheat went from 50 cents to $1.50 per bushel. Now Olmsted County farmers also had lower costs of transport by rail. And fertile loam soil helped make Olmsted one of the state's leading wheat-raising counties.

PUBLISHED BY J. E. WHITNEY, 171 THIRD STREET ST. PAUL, MINNESOTA.

Much wheat went out by rail, but three new mills existed by 1870 for local processing. The Olds and Fishback mill ran on the Zumbro near downtown. Ten blocks north, also on the Zumbro, John M. Cole had constructed a flour mill and milled 100,000 bushels of wheat between 1869 and 1870. About 10 blocks north of Cole's mill, at the falls on Cascade Creek, Abraham Harkins ran a gristmill that ground flour to return to the wheat farmer. In 1869 a gristmill on Bear Creek, a mile from town, ground flour while in another part of the building, a woolen mill carded wool, thereby giving farmers an additional local source of cash. In 1873 a million bushels of wheat came into Rochester. Some was shipped right out, but four mills exported 20,000 barrels of flour by rail.

Once the railroad arrived, merchants no longer needed to take farmers' oats or livestock as barter for store goods. Gone too were five months of business stagnation caused by the winter freeze on the Mississippi that would end steamboat service each year. Business was year-round, inventory turnover was quicker, and merchants carried smaller inventories since railcars could restock them within days. Selling for cash, not credit, was stressed. September 1870 advertisements in the *Rochester Post* trumpeted John Young's daily shipments of grocery items "from the Atlantic Cities" and J. Marquardt's return "from the Atlantic cities where he has bought an Extensive Stock of Merchandise!" Farm machinery came by rail. Dealers advertised threshing machines, mowers, wagons, and harvesters.

Eastern traveling salesmen or "drummers" came to drum up orders for wholesalers in Chicago or elsewhere. Salesmen needed hotel rooms, and several hotels sprang up: the Keystone, the Cook, the Steven's House. The first county courthouse became the Broadway House Hotel. Later, a three-story hotel changed names like a drummer changing trains: Pierce House, Commercial House, back to Pierce House, then Grand Union Hotel, and finally the New Rochester Hotel. Tourists also patronized these hotels, but traveling salesmen were their most reliable means of support.

The railroad, the new businesses it brought, and the increasing population led to other improvements. John R. Cook's First National Bank opened 10 weeks after the trains arrived. One of Minnesota's finest school buildings, the four-story brick Central School appeared in 1867–68. New churches and a new courthouse added towers and spires to form a city skyline. The population soared, from 1,424 in 1860 to 3,953 in 1870 to 5,103 in 1880. Fearing other cities' faster growth, some leaders felt the glass was half empty as well as half full.

John D. Blake & Company on Broadway competed to be the cheapest, highest-volume seller of dry goods by offering "One Price to All." The business depended on rail shipments of inventory, but Blake appealed to farmers' distrust of railroads in his advertisements. He became the plaintiff in one of Minnesota's most famous court cases, *John D. Blake v. Winona & St. Peter Railroad Company*. Rochester's businessmen and area farmers complained that the W&SP charged 15 cents per bushel to haul wheat 50 miles from Rochester to Winona but only 10 cents to take it 92 miles from Owatonna to Winona. Owatonna was the junction of two railroads, which competed for freight; Rochester had one railroad with no competitor.

On December 1, 1870, hundreds of farmers and local residents met in a hall to hear speeches against the W&SP. Dr. William W. Mayo was elected secretary. He introduced a successful resolution calling for "Civil Service and Revenue Reform" as well. The Rochester meeting led to an 1871 state law regulating railroads and setting maximum freight rates.

This page, top: First National Bank, 1892. This page, bottom: Broadway House Hotel, 1874. Opposite page: Chicago Great Western, circa 1910.

MALLET ENGINE WEIGHT 252 TONS LENGTH 82 FT TRACTIVE POWER 6...

The Blake case tested whether that law was constitutional. Five years later, the U.S. Supreme Court decided that a railroad was a public highway subject to such regulation; the W&SP had to charge Blake only 57 cents to bring him two bales of cotton cloth from Winona, not the dollar it wanted to charge.

Rochester thrived with the railroad, even if it feared that Owatonna might thrive more.

By October 1878, the Rochester and Northern Minnesota Railroad ran north of town to Zumbrota, but it was essentially a W&SP branchline. True competition arrived with the Chicago Great Western in 1900–03.

A railroad initially favored the local economy over outside businesses. Using railcars to export commodities or to order inventory was a simple proposition. It would take 30 years for businessmen marketing brand-name products nationwide to capture local markets.

The census of 1870 counted many craftsmen and small manufacturers in Rochester, including 53 carpenters, 14 masons, six blacksmiths, six shoemakers, four wagon shops, four harness shops, three brewers, three tinsmiths, two coopers, a machine shop, a plow shop, a sash and blind factory, a cigar maker, a gunsmith, a tanner, an upholsterer, a brick maker, and a carriage trimmer. Farm machinery manufacturers like McCormick were first to market through their local dealers offering farmers credit. Rochester had several such farm-implement dealers. Other industries were slow to follow suit.

Thirty-five years later, Rochester would benefit from Sears Roebuck's nationwide catalogue sales. In a fight against Kodak, Sears switched to the Conley Camera Company as its supplier, and Conley moved its factory to Rochester in 1904. Briefly, the Conley was called the Queen City camera—after Rochester's title of Queen City. These developments, however, were still in the future. In 1870 no Sears Roebuck, and few national brand names, existed.

A walk down Broadway, Rochester's main business street, in the 1880s revealed a rich variety of retail stores, craftsmen's shops, and small factories or workshops. The local still trumped the national.

The W&SP, a division of the Chicago & Northwestern Railroad, crossed Broadway between 8th and 9th Streets North. The passenger depot was a block west on Main Street, but most wooden warehouses, sheds, and elevators lining the two main tracks and assorted side tracks contained the raw commodities—the coal and lumber shipped in, and the grain, wool, and hides being shipped out. Another elevator stood a block north on 10th and Broadway. Within a block of the tracks were three lower-class hotels, some of whose customers may have been raw commodities themselves.

At 7th and Broadway, Harold Buttles's steam engines ground feed and powered a planing mill that produced doors, window frames, and window shades. His woodpiles filled half a block. Across the street, a cooper's shop made barrels for the flour mills and, a few steps east, Irving Fox made guns and hand grenades. A butcher sold meat at the corner of 6th and Broadway. Farther south, in the shopping district, banks occupied corner lots for greater visibility and proof they could afford higher rents or prices. Here, no clear zoning existed, and dwellings mixed with shops seemingly at random.

This page: Conley Camera Company, 1907. Opposite page, clockwise from left: Mueller & Company Grocers, 1893; Fox's Gun & Machine Shop, 1898; Northwestern Meat Market, 1908.

This page, clockwise from top: Broadway, 1890; Darling's Business College, circa 1887–95; Dick Russell Barber Shop, 1890. Opposite page: Schuster's brewery, date unknown.

At 5th and Broadway, a dozen men labored at the Northwestern Carriage Works manufacturing lumber wagons, spring wagons, and buggies. They turned out 100 annually. Another carriage maker, Thomas P. Hall, had a similar crew in his factory on the south side of the retail district. Across the alley from Northwestern, a shop made anvils and vises, and across the street, Fred Livermore employed 10 men at his foundry.

The retail district along Broadway featured two- to four-story brick buildings with awnings over street-level stores to block glaring morning or evening sunlight. Horses were tethered to hitching posts and rails on both sides of the street, but livery stables were on side streets, not this showcase one. Customers walked down the sidewalks to stores offering jewelry, drugs, boots and shoes, books and stationery, groceries, china, glassware, millinery, men's clothing, and cigars. Employees added to the crowds. Seven women worked at the two millinery shops. Blake hired six women for his clothing and dry goods store in the Heaney block near Zumbro and Broadway. In the rear of that three-story brick building was Darling's Business College, with an enrollment of 125 students, hopefully hard at work and not skipping class to shop.

Across Zumbro Street, the four-story brick Cook's Hotel was the city's centerpiece, with its high ceilings, its fireplaces of white marble, and its initial cost of $80,000 when constructed in 1869–70. A store owner and railroad investor before starting the First National Bank in 1864, Cook built up a sizeable fortune before he died in 1880. Five stores and his bank occupied the hotel's first floor.

The retail district continued one block south of 3rd Street, but the number of saloons increased to five as Broadway approached the south-end industrial area near the Zumbro's waterfall. The Olds and Fishback mill used waterpower as well as steam power. Not a gristmill, it ground flour to export. It employed seven men and produced 22,000 barrels per year. Southwest and upstream lay Henry Schuster's Union Brewery, also with seven workers. A scattering of livery stables, storage sheds, woodpiles, and dwellings half filled this industrial area, while the city fire hall kept vigilant watch over their fire-causing potentialities.

In 1882–83, Rochester was little different from hundreds of midwestern county seats and rail centers with 5,000 inhabitants. The city council met in a second-floor hall above the fire engines—to the disgust of the newly elected mayor, Dr. William W. Mayo, who stormed out of one meeting to protest such ramshackle accommodations. But Mayo and his city were about to encounter drastic change.

CHAPTER THREE

Selling Services to Visitors

Mayor William W. Mayo specialized in medicine, not politics, although his visible political role drew attention to his skill as a general practitioner. Dr. Mayo continued his political activities and his civic involvement in Rochester, just as this small city continued to manufacture goods, sell farm machinery, and function as the county seat. But Dr. Mayo was about to witness a dramatic expansion of his medical practice—one that would mean a dramatic expansion for the city as well. Surgical services were about to become the city's main product.

Rochester, 1900

In the 1870s, surgery was not highly esteemed. Most surgeries were amputations, antiseptic methods were not used in the United States, and postoperative infections were common. Operations were done in the patient's home or the doctor's office. Hospitals were feared as places people went to die. A new era was about to change all that, and Dr. Mayo assisted in that revolution.

A voracious reader, Mayo was courageous, willing to defy traditional wisdom, and eager to travel to learn new techniques. His first breakthrough came in gynecology. After traveling to Pennsylvania to talk to the Atlee brothers, who removed ovarian tumors, he attempted the risky operation in 1880. A Rochester newspaper hailed this success. Details of Mayo's operations were publicized in the papers, which helped him earn a reputation as the state's best ovarian surgeon.

Mayo performed surgeries in patients' homes, with his wife, Louise, and his teenage sons, William and Charles assisting him. William J. Mayo, "Dr. Will," earned his M.D. degree in 1883; Charles H. Mayo, "Dr. Charlie," in 1888. Both sons began practicing medicine with their father after they graduated. Eager readers and travelers for new knowledge, the brothers added new techniques for appendectomies, goiter removals, and antiseptic methods.

The Mayos' skills were tested by a natural disaster on August 21, 1883. Toward the end of a hot summer day, a tornado roared through the north end of Rochester and into downtown. At the intersection of Zumbro and Broadway, the Mayo brothers narrowly escaped death when the cyclone tore a large cornice off the Cook Hotel and flung it onto the front end of their horse-drawn buggy.

More than 150 houses were demolished, the railroad's facilities destroyed, 26 people killed, and more than 100 people injured. William W. Mayo treated the injured at a hotel; his sons, at the Mayo office. There was no hospital, except for the State Hospital for the Insane set up in 1879 to house alcoholics, senile people, the mentally ill, and the developmentally disabled.

A hospital came slowly. Mother Mary Alfred Moes of the Sisters of St. Francis felt the disaster demonstrated how much Rochester needed a hospital. Knowing only the poor or the terminally ill went to hospitals, the senior Mayo warned her, "Mother Superior, this city is too small to support a hospital." Rochester had only 5,000 residents. Yet her timing was right. The Mayos' high success rate in surgery could raise a hospital's reputation. A better hospital could help the Mayos achieve an even better success rate. She persisted.

The Catholic sisters worked for nothing and cut costs to the bone to save money to build a hospital and to survive the difficult early years. The three-story brick Saint Marys Hospital, with room for 45 patients, opened in September 1889. At one point, of 400 patients admitted, only two died. That survival rate brought more patients.

Rochester was small but well suited to house a family of innovative surgeons and a hospital. The railroad helped. Patients came by train to Saint Marys. The railroad gave free tickets to patients who could not afford them and gave a free rail pass to the Mayos.

William W. Mayo phased out his role in the medical practice in the 1890s and was no longer seeing patients by 1899, although he did advise his sons.

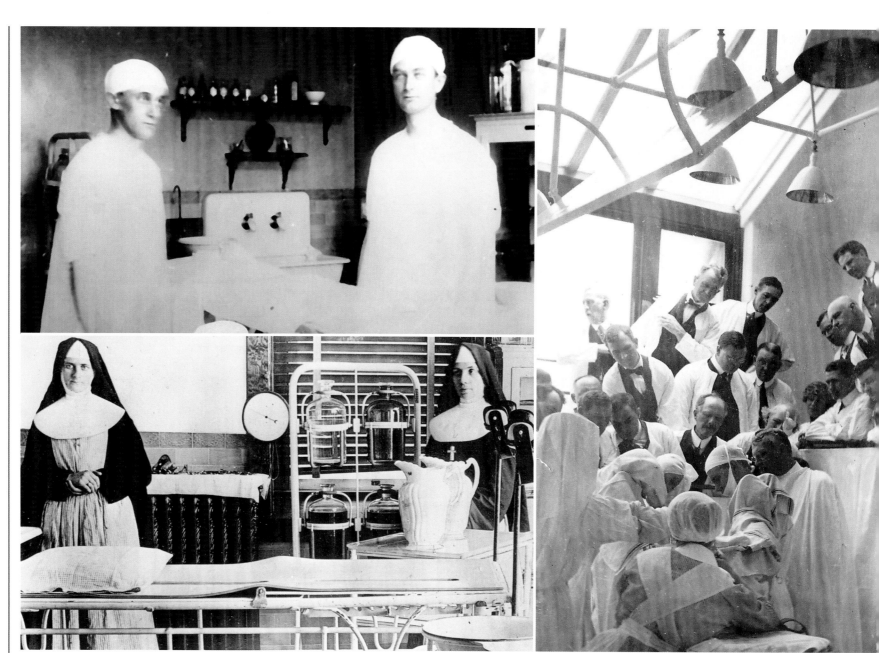

This page, clockwise from top left: Charles H. Mayo (left) and William J. Mayo (right) at Saint Marys Hospital, 1904; Charles H. Mayo operating at the Mayo Clinic, 1913; operating room at Saint Marys Hospital, 1893. Opposite page: First Mayo Clinic office, 1883.

Despite extensive reading and annual trips east to learn from other surgeons, the Mayo brothers had to master the new surgical techniques by doing large numbers of surgeries. With the best surgical reputations in the region and the only hospital there for a time, they performed thousands of surgeries during the 1890s. Their skill improved. Also, as doctors on the East Coast or in Europe pioneered surgeries for new diseases and different organs, the Mayos learned these techniques.

Practicing in a large city where there were other surgeons competing for patients would have forced the Mayos to specialize in one branch of surgery. As the sole doctors practicing at Saint Marys, however, they shared the surgical burden and added new surgical procedures as they developed. They added partnering doctors when the burden became too great.

It was a revolutionary time in medicine and surgery—like the computer revolution a century later—when one innovation grew out of the last. The use of anesthesia, for example, allowed more surgeries to be performed, but infection blocked progress until antiseptic and aseptic methods were used. When ruptures in the incision area occurred, surgery for hernias was developed. With each discovery, exact diagnosis became more crucial; diagnosis had mattered less when doctors could not

operate anyway. Invasive surgeries also required more skilled nursing for recovery. The Mayos and Saint Marys kept up with the innovations.

In 1905 William and Charles Mayo conducted nearly 4,000 operations at Saint Marys, which now had 175 beds. They had also added several doctors to their staff. Visiting surgeons now came to them and began calling this innovative private practice "the Mayo clinic at St. Marys hospital." Visitors formed an International Surgeons Club, rented meeting rooms, and discussed the day's operations each evening. The word "International" was eventually dropped, but foreign doctors still arrived. The Mayos gave impromptu narratives during the operations these visitors witnessed.

Doctors who needed an operation came to the Mayo brothers, and they referred their hardest cases to them. National publicity followed.

In 1914 the Mayo partnership moved to its own newly constructed building and began to call itself the Mayo Clinic. The sheer volume of cases forced a division of labor: surgeons, diagnosticians, lab analysts, and researchers. Different divisions for new specialties were added: orthopedics, neurology, thoracic surgery, dermatology, and pediatrics, among others. A central office handled the billing, accounting, record keeping, and other tasks. Rochester was home to an organizational innovation—the private group practice of medicine by many different cooperating specialists.

A clinic treating thousands of patients each year needed a sophisticated information storage and retrieval system. The Mayo Clinic needed that system three times over—for billing, for treating patients, and for advancing science by analyzing symptoms, treatments, and outcomes. Dr. Henry Plummer, who had joined the practice in 1901, designed a dossier system of patient files in 1907. He also set up a system that sent records by pneumatic tubes from one office to another.

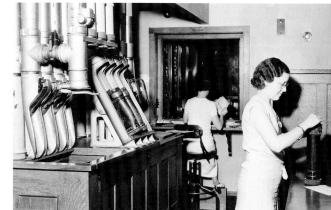

Dr. Will had said that the patient was not a wagon to be disassembled and fixed up piece by piece. The clinic had many specialists, but a patient had only one file, which went from one doctor to the next.

This page, top: Visitors in front of the Zumbro Hotel, 1922. This page, bottom: Mayo Clinic pneumatic tube system, 1934. Opposite page: Construction of a new Mayo Clinic building, circa 1913–14.

In 1915 a new Mayo Foundation for Medical Education and Research, endowed by the Mayo brothers, joined with the University of Minnesota to offer graduate education in medicine at the Mayo facilities. It was an honor to be chosen as a fellow to pursue graduate education at the Mayo Graduate School of Medicine. Graduates of medical schools from around the world applied in large numbers, and international students came to Rochester.

The growth at the clinic had attracted so many patients that it produced growth in the community. Saint Marys Hospital could no longer accommodate all the preoperative and postoperative patients, so hotels and convalescent homes entered that business.

John H. Kahler led a local revolution in the hotel business, which had to become a health care business in this city. The Mayo Clinic, whose fame had attracted more patients than its hospital could house, faced a bottleneck. Patients had to find rooms to await surgery and then to await full recovery before returning home. John Kahler worked hard to end this bottleneck.

The Kahler House hotel opened in 1907, with 60 beds for Mayo patients. By 1913 it had 140 rooms. In 1917 the Kahler Corporation was formed to build more hotels and more hospitals, including the Colonial Hospital, the Curie, the Stanley, the Samaritan, and the Worrall. In 1921 the new Kahler Grand Hotel opened with 210 hospital beds and 220 normal hotel beds. Dr. Will later praised John Kahler for doing more to advance the Mayo Clinic than "the rest of the citizens of Rochester put together."

Kahler facilities had to provide medical services for their special clientele. They had operating rooms and nurses. In 1918 the Kahler Corporation opened its first school for nurses. These Kahler services allowed the Mayo Clinic to focus on acute patient care and surgery.

In the 1920s, Kahler constructed a pedestrian subway to link various hotels and hospitals so patients would not have to brave Minnesota winters or downtown traffic.

People coming for medical treatment also needed other services: cafeterias, retail shops, luxury shops, ambulances, taxis, and pharmacies. An entrepreneur starting a business could count on a clientele of thousands of temporary residents. In 1919 Rochester's resident population of 13,000 had to accommodate 60,000 patients.

With the new medical and related services, the city's population increased from 6,843 in 1900 to 13,722 in 1920 to 20,614 in 1930. With the rise in population came cultural and sporting activities.

After the Civil War, Rochester became a center of horse breeding and was nicknamed "The Lexington of the Northwest" for a time. Horse racing flourished also. A wealthy migrant from Kentucky, Dan Heaney, was the leader in this pastime. He exported horses and built an opera house, Heaney Hall, in 1867 but spent his fortune in six years and left town.

Rochester had a public library and a city band in 1898. In 1901–02, the Metropolitan Theatre was built. Seating 800, the theater was one of the finest in the upper Midwest. Great actors and actresses like Maud Adams and Eva Tanguay appeared in the one-night shows that toured the nation in that premovie era.

In 1915 Rochester's Wide Awake Glee Club had some of Rochester's most prominent citizens as members, including John Kahler, Dr. Plummer and his wife, and three other medical couples.

By the early 20th century, the Mayos had placed philanthropy and cultural activities on a more substantial footing. Partly they did it so they could recruit talented physicians and surgeons to move to a small city in southeastern Minnesota. Skilled professionals could find positions almost anywhere and would examine the city's amenities before accepting a post at the Mayo Clinic. In 1904 the Mayos donated money to acquire a city park; in 1906, another park; and in 1915, a band shell. Innumerable other donations followed, including money for a swimming pool, a new library building, and the Mayo Civic Auditorium. An auditorium needed talent for its stage, and in 1921, Harold Cook formed the Philharmonic Orchestra. A Rochester Choral Society, Rochester Civic Theatre, and Rochester Symphonic Band followed later.

Public Library and Y. M. C. A., Rochester, Minn.

In 1915 Dr. Charles Mayo persuaded the Rochester school board to set up a two-year college program that became the Rochester Junior College in 1917. By 1923 it had more than 100 students. In 1927 the school began to offer the nation's first program for educating medical secretaries, a position for which there was clearly a local need.

As technology advanced, a small city needed more amenities to attract professionals. By the 1920s, an airport was one necessity. Business leaders took the initiative and secured a farm field, but air ambulance service for a medical services city demanded more than a rough, rural field. In 1928 the Mayo enterprises bought land for a larger, improved airfield closer to the clinic and hospitals. Scheduled commercial flights to Chicago and Minneapolis–St. Paul began that year.

That year Rochester also had a new skyscraper—a sure sign of urban status in the booming twenties. The Mayo Clinic's 15-story, $3 million Plummer Building could be seen towering over the city by 1928. It could be heard, too, for a bell tower added an extra four stories, and its 23-bell carillon rang out the hours of the day.

Rochester survived the depression of the 1930s. Patients and hotel guests declined in numbers, but providing medical services was a relatively stable business. On August 8, 1934, President Franklin D. Roosevelt came to Rochester to honor William J. and Charles H. Mayo, who received an American Legion award for treating disabled veterans free of charge. Five years later, the two brothers died within two months of each other.

The Mayos designed their clinic to last. A symbol of its continuity was its information storage and retrieval system designed by Dr. Plummer, which was used for several decades. Carts traveled on tracks carrying files in bulk, while individual files were blown through five miles of pneumatic tubes between various Mayo buildings.

The complexities of moving hundreds of thousands of records annually by track or by tube indicated that information science was in a primitive stage in the 1950s, as surgery had been a century earlier. Yet the Mayo Clinic's extensive investment in Rochester's civic and cultural life, and its record of business success there, would be a hopeful example to a computer firm thinking of moving there.

CHAPTER FOUR

Processing Information and Inventing Processes

Rochester "plays host to the world," its city slogan boasted in the 1940s. Rochester could also boast that it was a city of professionals. The percentage of its workforce in professional occupations was nearly triple the national average. It had a much higher percentage of adults with college degrees than the national average, a higher percentage of homes possessing radios than any Minnesota city (televisions were not yet common), and an unusually high figure for retail sales per capita. Its population in 1945 was estimated at 31,000, but on any one day about 8,000 visitors were in town, mainly visiting the Mayo Clinic and its allied hospitals. Staying eight days on average, visitors also patronized retail stores and restaurants.

Rochester, 1937

Two railroads provided passenger and freight service: the Chicago Great Western (CGW) and the Chicago & Northwestern (C&NW). Both railroads upgraded passenger service to compete with the automobile and the airplane. The C&NW redecorated its cars and improved its tracks to enable the streamlined Minnesota 400 to run at 80 miles per hour across southern Minnesota on the way east to Chicago. In January 1942, 2,000 people turned out at Rochester's train depot to see the new yellow and green train. At first a freight line, the CGW now added the nonstop Red Bird passenger train going north and south between Rochester and the Twin Cities. During World War II, troop trains rolled through Rochester as well.

The war changed Rochester's manufacturers. Conley Camera Company had become Waters Conley, which now subcontracted for work on missiles and an airplane gas gauge. After the war, Waters Conley manufactured instruments for the Mayo Clinic, including a cardiotachometer to measure heart rate, an oximeter to measure the blood's oxygen content, and a camera for use during surgery.

The Mayo Clinic and its affiliates continued to thrive during the 1940s. They contributed to the war effort by helping develop the "G" suit—an antiblackout suit for pilots—as well as other high-altitude devices for pilots. They attracted the 8,000 daily visitors who made the city much more than a county-seat, small-manufacturers' town. They supported the 65 hotels and 200 boarding and rooming houses in 1945.

In 1949 the Mayo Clinic hired Harry Blackmun, a St. Paul attorney, as its first legal counsel. Blackmun, whose office was in the clinic, attended surgeons' meetings, watched medical experiments, and heard doctors present their analytical papers. In 1950 two Mayo doctors, Edward C. Kendall and Philip S. Hench, won the

Nobel Prize in Physiology and Medicine for identifying cortisone and using it to treat rheumatoid arthritis. In the mid 1950s, the Mayo Clinic took part in the pioneering work in open-heart surgery.

Blackmun remained at the clinic for nine years. His major accomplishment was recruiting the Methodists to run the Kahler hospitals and setting up a legal framework for that transfer. As legal counsel, he attended postmortem examinations after the few deaths in surgery, including the first open-heart surgeries at Mayo in 1955. Blackmun left the clinic in 1959 when he was appointed an appellate judge. In 1970 he was appointed and confirmed as a U.S. Supreme Court justice. Before writing the majority opinion in the *Roe v. Wade* case (1973), Blackmun researched the legal and medical history of abortion at the clinic's Plummer Library. He based his opinion partly on the insights into the medical profession that he had gained at the Mayo Clinic.

The Mayo Clinic was serving thousands of patients whose complex medical problems had to be tackled on an individual basis, and the clinic had devised an information storage and retrieval system to accomplish its goals. Other firms that made or sold widgets, however, could get by on simpler systems that kept track of inventory, payroll, billing, and other accounting mathematics. The dominant company selling such machines was International Business Machines (IBM). By 1956 IBM had operations in 81 countries and had plants in Great Britain, France, Germany, and four other nations.

KACHYESTVO   UGLYA   OPRYEDYELY AYETSYA   KALORYIYNOSTJYU

This card is punched with a sample Russian language sentence (as interpreted at the top) in standard IBM punched-card code. It is then accepted by the 701, converted into its own binary language and translated by means of stored dictionary and operational syntactical programs into the English language equivalent which is then printed.

IBM specialized in punch-card machines, which read patterns on cards with punched holes representing numbers or letters. When Tom Watson Jr. took over as the head of IBM in 1956, the faster Univac computer, with its magnetic tape, electronic gear, vacuum tubes, and noisy operations, was altering computing technology. To compete, IBM invested billions in a successful drive to design its own electronic computer. Watson also began looking for a site for a new IBM plant in the Midwest, where labor costs were lower than those of IBM's home, Armonk, New York.

In 1955 Rochester businessmen and civic leaders seeking to attract businesses to the city formed Industrial Opportunities, Inc. (IOI), whose initials recalled the input-output shorthand of the computer industry. The businessmen of 1955–56 did not see that coincidence though, for computers were not yet the must-have tool they would later become. One coincidence that was noticed occurred when IOI men fired a toy cannon for their public drive downtown, impressing two IBM employees who happened to be in Rochester that day surveying possible cities for a new plant.

Unlike the 1880s, when the Mayo brothers were innovating new techniques in surgery, the 1950s were not favorable for an entrepreneur in a small midwestern city like Rochester to enter the computer industry. Computer technology was not advancing rapidly enough to give a genius upstart enough of an edge over the established firms. The only way for Rochester to gain entrance was to catch the eye of a giant like IBM.

IBM was seeking a medium-sized city with a population of 25,000 to 75,000 and features that would be attractive to its professional employees: great schools, recreational facilities, a vibrant civic life, high-class cultural institutions, and an absence of slums and racial or religious tension. On February 8, 1956, Watson announced that Rochester had been chosen as the site for IBM's new plant from a list of 80 cities. "We intend to be good neighbors to all of you in Rochester, and we think you will consider us an asset," he said.

The rise of the Mayo Clinic helped make Rochester an attractive choice for IBM and its professional employees. It also gave the new plant a sizeable nearby customer for medical-information products and services. Without Mayo, Rochester would not have had the minimum population (25,000), nor Mayo Civic Auditorium and other cultural institutions, nor excellent schools.

This page, top: IBM punch card, 1954. This page, bottom: IBM machine using punch cards, 1953. Opposite page: IBM's Rochester plant, 1958.

Twenty percent of IBM's Rochester employees were to be professionals. The Mayo Clinic would not compete with IBM for employees, for it hired doctors and nurses, not engineers and assembly-line workers—which would constitute 80 percent of IBM's anticipated workforce.

IBM was a "good neighbor" in designing the new plant as a campus, with plenty of open land surrounding the buildings northwest of the city. Still farmland, the 397-acre site stretched for nearly a mile on the west side of Highway 52. IBM commissioned famed architect Eero Saarinen to design the new plant. When it opened in 1958, the $8 million facility had more than 1,500 workers.

Initially, the plant manufactured the old punch-card technology: a numeric collator, an alphabetic collator, punch machines, and others. In the early 1960s, Watson invested billions in a bold project to design an integrated-circuit electronic computer to replace IBM's old machines—the ones Rochester made. Fortunately for Rochester, an IBM development laboratory was set up there in 1961. IBM Rochester could now make innovations as well as machines and create its destiny rather than only await word from IBM headquarters.

Watson's project led to the System/360 computer, a room-size mainframe. In 1969 Rochester's laboratory came out with the System/3, the first computer developed exclusively at Rochester. A midrange small-business computer, the System/3 moved from punch cards to magnetic disk storage. Customers liked it. High sales figures gave the Rochester plant an added feeling of security. Mainframes had higher status in IBM and were made in upstate New York, but midrange computers proved the better long-range choice for Rochester.

From the start, the development lab worked on medical electronics, an obvious move to sell to nearby Mayo. The new innovation in the 1960s was the IBM Surgical Monitoring System, which allowed a surgeon to check on a patient's blood pressure, EKG readings, and other key signs. In 1973 IBM set up a computer link between the Mayo Clinic and Saint Marys Hospital. The sterile environment needed for making disk drives paralleled the requirements for an operating room, and some sharing of techniques may have occurred.

While a small firm might survive by specializing in computer services for the health care industry, a huge plant like IBM Rochester needed a broader customer base. In the 1970s, IBM Rochester developed and manufactured "upward compatible" midrange computers—the desk-size System/32 with a floppy disk, the larger System/34 with its

This page, top: Circuit analysis at IBM Rochester, 1958. This page, bottom: IBM Rochester's System/3 computer, 1973. Opposite page: IBM Rochester's System/36 computer, 1983.

work-station design, and the System/38, the top of this line—raising the plant's workforce to more than 6,000 by 1980. In 1983 came the System/36, and more than 100,000 were sold in three years. These midrange computers proved to have more stability in sales than did mainframes and microcomputers, or even personal computers, which ran into fierce competition in the late 1980s and early 1990s.

IBM Rochester facilitated the city's growth. While the shops for Mayo clients still thrived downtown, along the pedestrian subway system, and at street level, new shopping centers were built on the city's outskirts for city residents and the new IBM workers—Northgate and Miracle Mile at the intersection of highways 14 and 52; Apache Mall, the first indoor enclosed mall in the area; and Crossroads at the intersection of highways 14 and 63. Major department stores such as Dayton's, JCPenney, Sears, and Montgomery Ward located at the shopping centers or downtown.

This page: Apache Mall,
circa 1969. Opposite
page, left: Corncob
water tower. Opposite
page, right: Last
passenger train leaving
Rochester, 1963.

In 1972 Rochester's workforce was allocated fairly evenly, with 4,300 at the Mayo Clinic, 4,100 at IBM, 2,300 at the two main hospitals (Saint Marys and Methodist), and 1,000 at the canning factory of Libby, McNeill & Libby. The latter kept alive the city's tradition of agriculture-related industries. The factory's corncob-shaped water tower served as a landmark and a reminder of Rochester's farming past. In occupational status, the city's workforce was not split evenly but was nearly 40 percent managerial or professional.

The railroad, however, did not prosper. The last passenger train left the city on July 23, 1963—the victim of interstate highways and airplane service. Interstate 90 was to be built shortly just six miles south of Rochester. In 1968 the C&NW acquired the CGW. Abandonment of tracks began. The CGW tracks north and south of the city were gone by the end of 1977. Even freight service was affected, as high-tech businesses like IBM did not ship their high-value products out by rail.

By contrast, the computer industry did increase the demand for higher education in Rochester, which was already high due to the need of a professional workforce. The University of Minnesota began offering continuing education courses in Rochester in 1966, in addition to the ongoing graduate program in medicine at the Mayo Clinic. The university's Institute of Technology offered televised versions of its courses at the IBM plant. The school also offered master's degrees in nursing, computer science, and electrical engineering—fields clearly relevant to Rochester's main employers and, thus, to their workers seeking promotion. Winona State University began to offer nursing classes in Rochester in 1974.

The Mayo Clinic did not fear being superseded by some new technology, as the railroads did. And, it had an excellent reputation and name recognition. Celebrity patients helped. In January 1969, the *Wall Street Journal* ran a front-page article about Mayo, comedian Jack Benny's checkup there in 1965, and television host Ed Sullivan's visit a year later. Yet, most Mayo patients by far were average midwesterners. In the 1970s, the clinic's executives began to worry that past rates of growth in patient numbers could not be sustained. In 1983 the Mayo board approved a plan to expand by building new clinics in Arizona and Florida, where large numbers of senior citizens required medical services.

Just as the canning factory and its water tower reminded Rochester residents of their farming past, the Zumbro River's periodic floods recalled the city's original identity as the site of waterfalls. On July 5, 1978, some six inches of rain fell. The area's many brooks and creeks rapidly fed the runoff into the Zumbro, as they had with the runoff from melting glaciers millennia earlier. The next day, the stream reached 23 feet above flood stage. The raging waters cut off electricity to the two main hospitals, which had to rely on their emergency generators. The waters flooded some shopping centers, knocked out the city's sewer system, and caused $40 million in damages.

Nearly 125 years of human occupancy had created an extensive infrastructure—streets, highways, railroads, skyscrapers, shopping centers, and residences—but had not changed the area's underlying geophysical structure as a collection basin for water. Two new fields—surgery and computer technology—had brought an influx of highly educated professionals; however, the Zumbro would flood a neurosurgeon's or programmer's basement as readily as a blacksmith's.

Rochester recovered, planned for a series of levees and other flood-control measures, passed a 1 percent sales tax to finance them, and then awaited federal and state legislation to aid it in its efforts. The city would survive and thrive by containing the Zumbro.

This page, top: One of the Mayo Clinic's famous patients, Mickey Mantle, 1966. This page, bottom: Flooded parking lot, 1978. Opposite page: Downtown after the flood, 1978.

CHAPTER FIVE

Integrating Services and Information in a Global Age

The information revolution of the 1980s and 1990s aided one of Rochester's key employers, IBM, and did not harm the other, the Mayo Clinic and its allied hospitals. As was the case a century earlier, medical and surgical services still placed a premium on nurses' and doctors' personal skills and knowledge. Patients had to be diagnosed and treated one at a time in a personal manner, not in an assembly-line way that could be computerized. Patients would still travel long distances to obtain the services of the Mayo Clinic. The information revolution did not change those facts.

Rochester, 2007

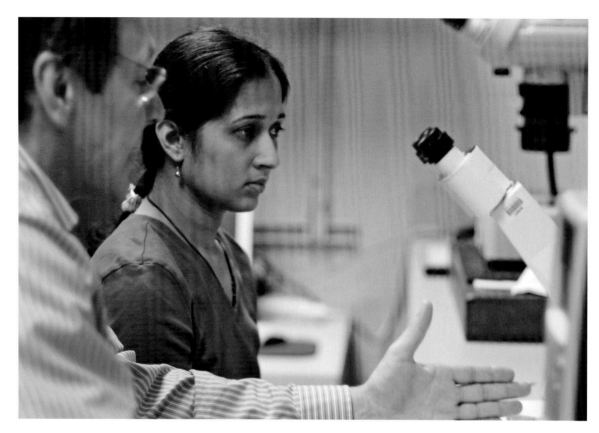

The Mayo Clinic did make changes at the margins, so to speak, of its basic clinical practice. In 1983 it began issuing the *Mayo Clinic Health Letter*. In less than two years, the newsletter's circulation grew to more than 140,000 subscribers, who paid $24 annually to receive tips for good health and news on recent advances in medicine. The clinic expanded its classroom educational mission as well. By 1989 the Mayo Graduate School was offering Ph.D. degrees on its own, apart from the University of Minnesota, and the Mayo Medical School was offering M.D. degrees. The Mayo School of Continuing Medical Education carried on the clinic's long tradition of sharing Mayo research and techniques to help doctors improve their skills.

That research was often of international importance. In 1992 a Mayo study of bone loss among Olmsted County residents led to the identification of osteoporosis as a disease rather than a normal part of the aging process.

In the 21st century, the clinic launched an online magazine, *Discovery's Edge*, dedicated to Mayo research. In the late 1990s, the medical records system at Mayo was computerized.

IBM, on the other hand, was vulnerable to its competitors' increasing role in the information revolution. That vulnerability did not at first threaten IBM Rochester or its specialty of midrange computers.

As IBM shifted some operations overseas, IBM Rochester employees learned to work with plants around the globe—disk drive plants in England, Germany, and Japan as well as IBM translation sites that could adapt midrange computers and their software to foreign languages. Typically, some 50 foreign language versions of the new software would be ready to go when the English version was announced.

IBM Rochester's workforce topped 7,000 by 1985, three times what IBM had promised 30 years earlier. Throughout the giant corporation, this branch plant was jokingly called "Fortress Rochester" for its employees' team spirit and close-knit innovation as well as their resistance to transferring to higher-status New York sites.

Nationally and internationally, however, IBM had grown a bit complacent and inflexible. Its engineers designed computers *they* liked, in secret labs off-limits to customers, whose wishes might not be heeded even if they were known. IBM computers didn't talk to each other. IBM engineers didn't talk to customers. They felt they didn't have to, for IBM dominated the small- to midsized business market.

This page: IBM Rochester's AS/400 computer, circa 1988–90. Opposite page: IBM Rochester facility.

In the 1980s, that changed. Customers insisted that their mainframes, midrange computers, and personal computers talk to each other. A secret IBM project to get four labs to design a new midrange computer to replace five existing ones had failed. The five IBM systems, two of which were made in Rochester, continued competing against each other, and they were all becoming outdated. If Rochester did not find a new midrange product to make and sell by the summer of 1988, it would be a plant without a mission.

In response, IBM Rochester began working on the "Silverlake Project," named after Rochester's downtown lake that, because it never freezes, is the winter home of thousands of Canada geese. Just as improbable was success in writing seven million lines of programming code, making a new computer by combining two older incompatible ones, and doing it in half the normal development time.

Headquarters allowed IBM Silverlake to operate as a small business, bypass corporate red tape, share secrets with customers, and ask customers for ideas. Silverlake beat the odds and introduced the AS/400 computer in June 1988. As a result, IBM Rochester won the coveted Malcolm Baldrige National Quality Award in 1990, an award created by Congress to recognize American businesses for achievements in quality and performance.

Ironically, the zeal of "Fortress Rochester" employees ended up improving the entire corporation—the plant became a prototype for the renewal of IBM in the mid to late 1990s. The IBM Rochester workforce reached a peak of 8,100 in 1990–91. The AS/400 proved an immensely popular midrange computer.

Another factor that enabled Silverlake to succeed was IBM's focus on educating its workforce. IBM spent 5 percent of its payroll on training and teaching its employees. In 1987 alone, the Education Department at IBM Rochester had more than 35,000 classroom days of instruction. It hired faculty from local colleges to teach employees, and this was a boost for the city's higher education providers—Rochester Community and Technical College (RCTC), Winona State University–Rochester, and the University of Minnesota Rochester.

In 1994 these institutions moved to an eastside location called University Center Rochester (UCR). This step forward was the fruit of work by local volunteers, including retired employees from the Mayo Clinic and IBM. Rochester still sought the state legislature's approval and funding for its own four-year university, but that goal was blocked for the time being by a statewide opinion that Minnesota had too many college campuses.

This page: IBM's Blue
Gene supercomputer.
Opposite page:
Minnesota corn farmer.

At UCR, students could earn undergraduate degrees in computer science, nursing, accounting, business administration, and other fields—or a master's degree in nursing. They could earn two-year degrees and certificates in technical skills useful to local employers. In 1991 Riverland Technical College was started to handle these programs, while RCTC offered the first two years of general education requirements for students who wanted to pursue a bachelor's degree. UCR would also become the site of Saint Mary's University of Minnesota Schools of Graduate and Professional Programs.

The community faced a major educational task with the arrival of hundreds of refugees from Southeast Asia in the 1970s and 1980s. The public school district began to teach English as a second language to refugees and their children. The Rochester International Association (RIA) and Intercultural Mutual Assistance Association (IMAA) were both formed in the early 1980s. The RIA held a World Festival each year to show the crafts, foods, clothing, and culture of various nationalities, while the IMAA instructed newcomers in basic self-help skills.

In 1984 the Federal Bureau of Prisons bought the site of the former Rochester State Hospital and converted it to a Federal Medical Center to provide medical care to prison inmates. The center would eventually become one of Rochester's top employers.

With its population on the rise, Rochester undertook a major rebuilding of its downtown in 1987–89. The final federal approval of flood control measures ensured that foreseeable flood levels on the Zumbro River would no longer threaten downtown. A combination luxury hotel, office building, and shopping center called Center Place served as the anchor for a new downtown. The Mayo Clinic erected a new education building.

In 1993 *Money* magazine named Rochester the best place to live in America out of the nation's 300 biggest metro areas. It scored high in health care but also in a low crime rate and a good economy. Rochester's population had grown from 57,890 in 1980 to 70,745 in 1990.

IBM's financial losses in the early 1990s, however, resulted in the layoff of 3,000 employees at IBM Rochester by 1995. Rapidly accelerating global competitiveness in the computer industry in the 1990s pushed IBM Rochester to create new innovations and close partnerships with spin-off companies. Between 2002 and 2004, IBM helped develop the Blue Gene supercomputer, which for a time was the world's fastest supercomputer.

In the competitive environment of the 1990s, IBM sometimes sold off a segment of its business or outsourced production. Yet outsourcing opened up opportunities for IBM employees willing to leave their jobs to start spin-off companies. Three former IBM managers formed Rochester Software Connection in 1989 to produce software for the AS/400 computer. Another firm, ShowCase, was started by a former IBM manager who wanted to sell software that would link Microsoft Windows to the AS/400. Pemstar was also founded by IBM employees who saw the early 1990s layoffs coming and started their own company partly to stay in Rochester. Pemstar, which was acquired by Texas-based Benchmark Electronics in 2007, is now one of the city's largest employers.

When the Milken Institute released its 1999 study of "America's High-Tech Economy"—an examination of how well metropolitan areas had performed in creating a high-tech economy—Rochester topped the list, with a concentration of high-tech businesses that was 5.5 times the national average.

IBM, plus the many spin-off and start-up companies in information technology, helped increase Rochester's population to an estimated 100,000 in 2007, establishing Rochester as Minnesota's third-largest city.

Rochester looks forward to a prosperous future, building on the solid foundations of past growth and adding new pieces that best fit those foundations. In doing so, Rochester remains a city of professionals, with nearly 47 percent of its workforce in the professional or management class in 2000. Today the Mayo Clinic and IBM anchor the city's economy, employing about 30,000 workers and 4,400 workers, respectively.

Still, the agricultural tradition remains. Seneca Foods Corporation, of New York, cans the area's vegetables, especially corn and peas. Pace Dairy Foods, of Rochester; Kemps, of St. Paul; and Associated Milk Producers, of New Ulm, turn out dairy products like cheese at local branches.

The manufacturing and craftwork of the late-19th-century railroad era also continues. There are some 150 manufacturers in the region today. Crenlo, which began in 1951 as a manufacturer of tractor cabs, expanded its line of products to metal enclosures for computer hardware in 1957 after IBM requested some metal fabricating work. Today Crenlo is one of

Rochester's 10 biggest employers. Other leading manufacturers include Tuohy Furniture Corporation, of Chatfield, and Halcon, of Stewartville, both of which produce furniture. Rochester Medical Corporation, of Stewartville, makes medical devices, Gauthier Industries, of Rochester, produces metal parts, and McNeilus Corporation, of Dodge Center, manufactures refuse truck bodies and mobile ready-mix concrete mixer trucks.

The hospitality skills and services that John Kahler did so much to improve in the early 20th century are today flourishing in a city that offers about 5,000 rooms in more than 50 hotels and motels. The corporation that owns the Kahler hotels, California-based Sunstone Hotel Investors, is now Rochester's 10th-largest employer.

Some 165 restaurants provide meals for visitors. Art galleries, concert halls, historic sites, nature centers, parks, and theaters provide cultural and recreational opportunities. Commercial airline flights from Chicago, Detroit, and Minneapolis arrive daily at Rochester International Airport. About 1.5 million visitors come to Rochester each year.

This page: Rendering of the planned Minnesota BioBusiness Center. Opposite page: Concept for the new University of Minnesota Rochester campus.

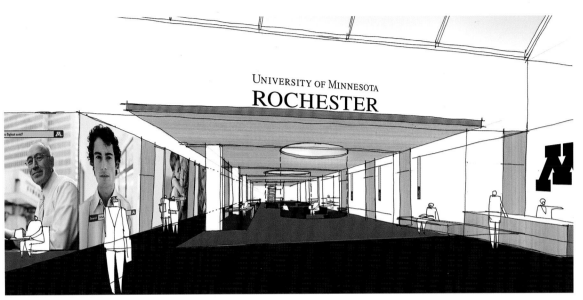

UNIVERSITY OF MINNESOTA
ROCHESTER

Today Rochester is working to attract firms in the new bioscience industry to expand its economic base further. The city is already home to the Minnesota Partnership for Biotechnology and Medical Genomics, an ongoing partnership between the University of Minnesota and the Mayo Clinic. The Mayo-University partnership is building a facility downtown, and it has grant monies from the state to distribute to researchers.

Plans have begun for the Minnesota BioBusiness Center downtown, a facility that will offer office and lab space for bioscience companies. Companies locating in the center will have a prime location near the Minnesota Partnership for Biotechnology and Medical Genomics, as well as IBM's facility for the Blue Gene computer, which can perform the calculations needed for the analysis of proteins and the human genome.

Synergism has already scored one success—in 2006 the University of Minnesota and the state government agreed to develop a four-year university campus in Rochester. The fears of duplicating other campuses' missions have been partly laid to rest by the bioscience mission contemplated for this school of the future. As part of the expansion, the university will create a new campus, along with new and expanded academic programs and research partnerships. A master campus planning group will convene in 2007.

These new developments in Rochester would hardly be possible without the city's long history of innovation. Like the geological layers deposited millennia earlier, Rochester's economic layers remain to support a unique urban society that draws entrepreneurs and visitors from around the globe.

PART TWO

CHAMPIONS OF COMMERCE

Profiles of Companies and Organizations

PROFILES OF COMPANIES AND ORGANIZATIONS

Agribusiness and Food Processing

Pace Dairy Foods

Owned and operated by the Kroger Company, this cheese-processing plant produces both natural and processed cheese in some 500 sizes, types, and flavors. It annually ships 137 million pounds of product, offering consumers in 31 states a huge selection of quality cheese.

Above left: Pace Dairy Foods operates out of Rochester, where it can take advantage of the region's large supply of milk for cheese making. Above right: Pace produces 100 million pounds of cheese a year for Kroger stores.

In the late 1960s, Kroger Company began a program to provide cheese to its stores. Its research showed that southeastern Minnesota would be the approximate center for the highest milk supply in the nation well into the 1980s, making Rochester a desirable location for long-term cheese production and procurement. This, along with the availability of competent labor and the cooperation of city officials, sold Kroger on the Rochester site for its dairy. Kroger began building a cheese processing plant in 1972, and by 1974 Pace Dairy Foods was operating.

Keeping Pace with Demand

In 1971—its first full year of operation—Pace supplied its parent company with 9,785,000 pounds of cheese, about 36 percent of the cheese sold in Kroger stores. In 1977 Pace supplied 51,628,000 pounds of cheese, almost 58 percent of the chain's cheese sales. Today those figures have risen considerably.

Pace employs some 300 full-time workers, produces 100 million pounds of cheese each year, and annually ships about 137 million pounds of finished product. Its 143,000-square-foot plant has two departments: natural cuts and processed cheese. Each department runs three shifts and maintains a full sanitation crew on the third shift. In all, the dairy labels some 500 sizes, types, and flavors of natural and processed cheese.

Aged for Success

Pace credits its success largely to Kroger's superstore concept and the grocer's ability to merchandise and sell the cheese that Pace makes. Kroger also recognized the potential in the cheese industry for the individually wrapped slice (IWS). In the late 1970s, Kroger and Pace pioneered equipment that combined manufacturing and wrapping into one operation. The IWS was well-received by modern, on-the-go consumers who value convenience.

Pace Dairy Foods aligns itself with its parent company's core values: honesty, respect, inclusion, diversity, safety, and integrity. It continues to offer consumers a superior selection of quality cheeses at an excellent value.

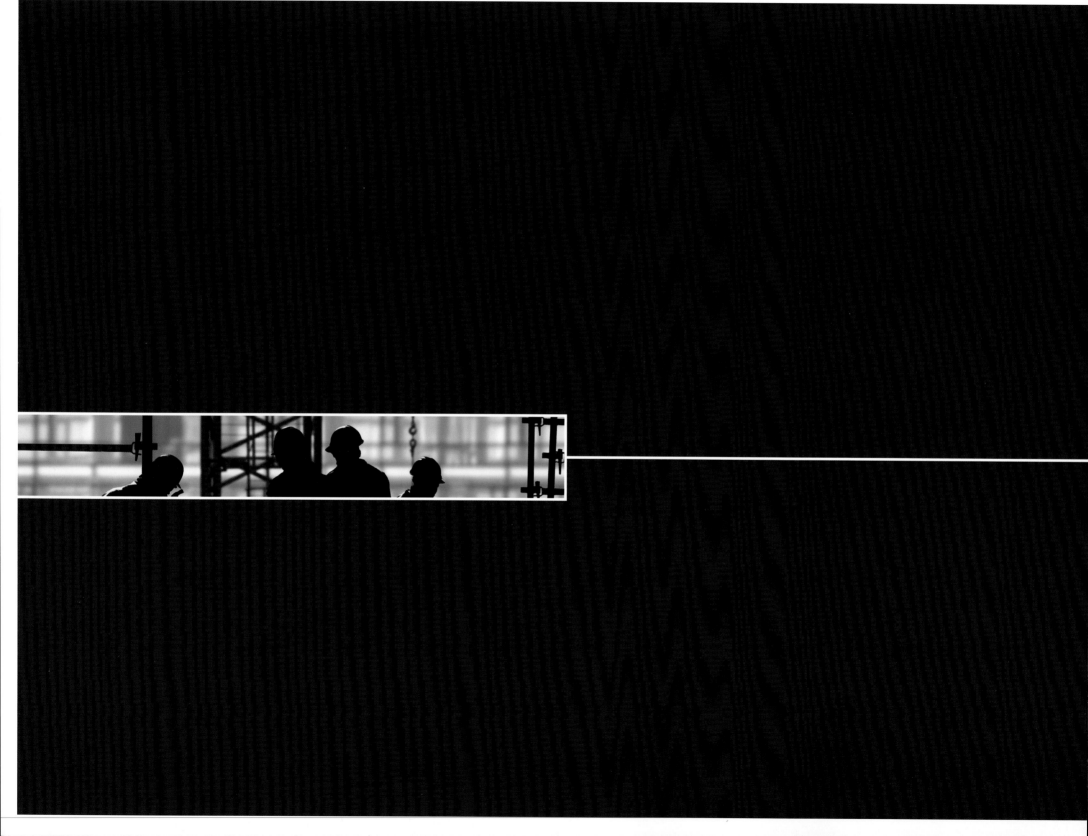

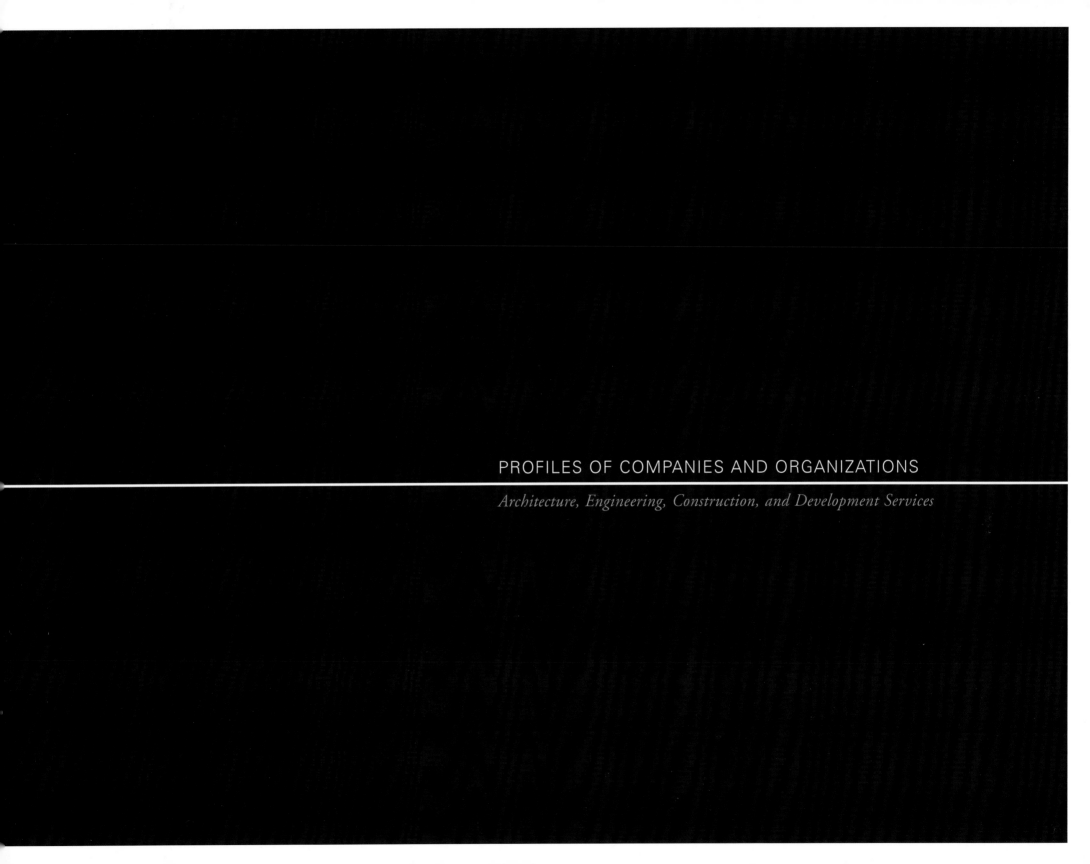

PROFILES OF COMPANIES AND ORGANIZATIONS

Architecture, Engineering, Construction, and Development Services

McGhie & Betts, Inc.

Established in 1946, this multidisciplinary Rochester firm is recognized as one of the leaders in the civil engineering, environmental, surveying, and planning professions in the upper Midwest. Using smart growth and green building practices, it develops projects for clients in the private and public sectors.

McGhie & Betts, Inc. was founded in 1946 as a civil engineering and land surveying firm servicing primarily southern Minnesota. Over the years it has evolved into a firm that integrates civil and geotechnical engineering, planning, environmental services, construction material testing, landscape architecture, and ground and air transportation consulting, with offices serving clients throughout the upper Midwest.

The firm's team of professionals has been a leader in providing innovative approaches to project design in both the public and private sectors. Conservation design, smart growth projects, and green building development concepts are now standard.

The success of McGhie & Betts is attributable to its large and diverse repeat clientele and dedicated staff. Success is also based on practicing the firm's mission statement: "McGhie & Betts is committed to the highest quality of service in private development, public works, and the natural environment by understanding the needs of our clients and assisting

them to envision and achieve their goals through the creative and innovative use of our human and technical resources."

The Firm

Headquartered in Rochester with branch offices in Northfield, Minnesota, and Bozeman, Montana, the firm continues with steady growth after doubling in size in the late 1980s and the 1990s.

The strength of the firm is its integration of professional disciplines to provide a full-service, one-stop consulting firm for clients in the public and private sectors. McGhie & Betts has expanded into two companion companies: McGhie & Betts Environmental Services, Inc. and McGhie & Betts Transportation Services, Inc.

McGhie & Betts Environmental Services was established in 1990 to provide a wide range of services from wetland mitigation and asbestos abatement to indoor air quality and environmental assessments. The staff now includes geologists, soil scientists, and environmental engineers, in addition to a range of other environmental specialists.

McGhie & Betts Transportation Services was formed in 2006 to provide clients with surface and air transportation planning, design, and construction. Its office is at the Rochester International Airport.

Client Focus

McGhie & Betts serves public sector clients such as airports, medical and educational institutions, municipalities, townships, counties, and state and federal agencies. Public projects involve wastewater treatment, water supply, roads, sewer systems, airports, transportation, and other infrastructure. One of the largest public sector projects is the Rochester International Airport. McGhie & Betts was instrumental in the siting of the airport in the late 1950s and has been a consulting firm for the airport since 1946.

Private sector clients include residential developers, commercial and industrial developers, architects, and contractors. Projects range from large residential developments to shopping centers. In the private sector, McGhie & Betts approaches residential and commercial

projects—urban or rural—with conservation design principles. Zumbro Haven, nestled in the hills near Lake Zumbro in Oronoco Township, is one example of residential conservation design. Another is Mayo Woodlands in Rochester Township, southwest of Rochester. This 470-acre development mixes prairie and woodland lots with on-site community wastewater treatment systems next to a 270-acre conservation parcel. For the Harvestview project in northwest Rochester, McGhie & Betts incorporated smart growth and green building principles. This 320-acre mixed-use development integrates neighborhoods, businesses,

public schools, and city storm water ponds with bike paths and pedestrian-friendly corridors.

Prairie Crossing is a large community on the north side of Rochester that will consist of more than 700,000 square feet of structures connected by an outdoor walking mall called Prairie Village. This project is designed to incorporate an existing 100-year-old oak savannah forest.

Rochester, Minnesota, is home to the world-renowned Mayo Clinic, one of the fastest-growing medical centers in the United States. McGhie & Betts has provided consulting services for a wide range of Mayo Clinic facilities since 1946.

McGhie & Betts has a diversified staff that combines efforts in completing projects, usually without the need for outsourcing portions of the work.

Strength of the Firm

McGhie & Betts has two major strengths. The first is knowledge of the marketplace, which the firm has put into practice by working directly with communities and private clients in Minnesota, Iowa, South Dakota, Wisconsin, Illinois, and Michigan. The second is communication. Communication is critical in a multidiscipline consulting firm, and each department works together to

understand clients' goals, listen to their concerns, and deliver the results they want.

McGhie & Betts has a history of completing quality projects. The firm has prepared and received the approval of more than 20,000 acres of residential, commercial, and industrial development since 1977. McGhie & Betts has a 97 percent project approval rate. Many municipal agencies have consulted the firm for large and small projects throughout the region.

The firm's technical skills, licensed professional engineers, land surveyors, landscape architects, soil scientists, certified planners, registered environmental specialists, and excellent reputation—it has an 85 percent repeat client base—are other strengths that create success.

Left, top: McGhie & Betts has integrated planning, engineering, and surveying in its transportation solutions since 1946. Left, bottom: The firm's projects include Zumbro Haven in Oronoco Township, surrounded by woodlands, steep terrain, and Lake Zumbro. The 111-acre site includes 45 single-family lots, community open space, and rural roadways. Above right: Another mixed-use community project is Prairie Crossing, which is connected by Prairie Village (shown here)—an outdoor mall with shopping, culinary, and entertainment districts. A ribbon of water links the plaza area to the park.

Woodruff Company

This longtime successful Rochester enterprise, a full-service wholesale distributor, remains dedicated to supplying customers with plumbing, heating, and related products with friendly, efficient service at fair, competitive prices that profit all concerned.

Above: Woodruff Company was founded by James Woodruff in Rochester, Minnesota, in 1947. Right, all photos: Today, the company's Rochester headquarters is an 85,000-square-foot complex that includes the Showroom Idea Center (top), which is an expansive display area—open to the public—with stylish displays of products for both new construction and remodeling projects, available through contractors. Branch facilities of Woodruff Company are located in Austin (center) and Winona, Minnesota (bottom).

The vision of Woodruff Company is to be the leading company serving its market segments. The company's mission is to supply its customers with plumbing, heating, and closely related products, providing prompt and friendly service at fair and competitive prices that are profitable for all concerned. Its focus is customer satisfaction through continual improvement. Its team member commitment to customer service is validated by its taglines "Your full-service wholesaler since 1947" and "Meeting your needs."

The company's founder, James Woodruff, worked with his father in distribution in the Twin Cities during the 1930s, and after World War II he decided to start his own business. He opened Woodruff Company in 1947 in Rochester, Minnesota, to supply contractors who were installing plumbing, heating, and air-conditioning. The business succeeded, and branches were established in Austin in 1958 and Winona in 1989.

In the company's early postwar days, businesses were in the process of converting their production from war

materials back to consumer goods, so manufactured goods were in short supply. Woodruff Company's greatest challenge became obtaining a sufficient stock of products to serve its customers' needs. Today, by contrast, when goods are readily available from manufacturers and many companies market plumbing and heating products, Woodruff Company's greatest challenge is to maintain its market share and continually gain new customers, both contractors and consumers.

In the early 1970s, following college and work experience elsewhere, the founder's sons, Jim Woodruff and John Woodruff, joined their father in the company. Today they serve as president and vice president, respectively. James Woodruff (1914–2001) supported Lourdes High School and helped start Lourdes Foundation, which assists students with tuition and faculty members with extra development programs. Woodruff Company supports Rochester Youth Hockey, financing scoreboards in the Graham Arenas, located in the Olmsted County Fairgrounds, across from the Woodruff Company's Rochester location.

From the 1960s to the 1980s, Woodruff Company maintained a Builders Division, selling appliances, cabinets, and related products to home builders. Since then it has concentrated on plumbing, heating, and air-conditioning.

Today Woodruff Company markets many plumbing and heating lines, including Kohler plumbing fixtures, MAAX Aker bath bays, Delta and Moen faucets, American Water Heaters, Goodman and Luxaire heating and air-conditioning, and Water-Right water-treatment systems. Its customer segments include contractors and commercial, residential, government, and manufacturing organizations. In Rochester, Woodruff Company offers a Kohler-registered showroom selling products for both new construction and remodeling. Showroom sales are usually made through contractors.

Woodruff Company points out how the function of a wholesale distributor such as itself brings efficiency and cost savings to the marketplace. Woodruff Company buys from about 400 suppliers and sells to about 600 customers. Without a distributor, this could mean

400 times 600, or 240,000, paths of interaction. With the function of a distributor, these potential paths of interaction are reduced from 240,000 to just 400 plus 600, or 1,000, paths—making possible a more manageable and cost-effective way of conducting business.

Woodruff Company
Your full service wholesaler since 1947
Meeting your needs

woodruffcompany.com

Ellerbe Becket, Inc.

Iconic in its stature and creations, this Minnesota-based architecture, engineering, and construction firm is recognized worldwide for its expertise in designing virtually every type of building—from health-science to sports facilities, and from universities to urban mixed-use complexes.

Since 1909, when it was established, Ellerbe Becket, Inc. has been a key force in shaping the skyline of Rochester. This leading design firm, headquartered in Minneapolis, has built a solid foundation with Mayo Clinic and the City of Rochester. Throughout its history, Ellerbe Becket has been committed to designing buildings in Rochester and throughout the world that contribute to the communities it serves.

Ellerbe Becket's success and longevity can be attributed to its collaborative approach and its focus on innovation and understanding clients' needs. For nearly a century, these values have enabled the firm to deliver inspired solutions and designs to meet even the most challenging client requirements. Today, Ellerbe Becket provides expertise in architecture, interior design, and construction along with mechanical, electrical, and structural engineering to clients in all 50 states and 20 countries worldwide.

Mayo Clinic: An Example of Present and Future Innovation

From Mayo Clinic's original 70,000-square-foot building in 1914 to the 1.5-million-square-foot Gonda Building, Ellerbe Becket has been intricately involved in Mayo Clinic's evolution, helping it constantly improve health care delivery and better meet patient needs with improved facilities.

Over the past decade, Mayo Clinic has pursued a series of projects to reintegrate its clinical practice into interconnected facilities. The Gonda Building is the centerpiece of that effort. This project challenged Ellerbe Becket to design and create a building that would have a useful life of at least 100 years. In response, Ellerbe Becket made the Gonda Building innovative and state-of-the-art, with a flexible infrastructure framework and durable, high quality materials. The new building provides a new "front door" to the storied institution and also ushers in a new level of patient care. The design directly connects the clinical practice areas to each of the existing Mayo Building's 18 levels and to the rest of the Mayo campus via skyways and subways.

Rochester native John Waugh, AIA, who is also the son of a Mayo Clinic surgeon, has a lifelong connection to Mayo Clinic. As Ellerbe Becket's design and planning principal for Mayo Clinic, he has spent more than 30 years working on the clinic's projects—from renovations to today's practice integration projects.

Waugh says of Ellerbe Becket's work on the 20-story Gonda Building, "The process was unique, as is the finished project. We designed the building to provide a framework for change and growth. Mayo can eventually build an additional 10 stories, and with its flexible infrastructure, the building can accommodate future clinical services, patient beds, or laboratory modules. It is probably the first health care facility designed and constructed as a super high-tech, tenant fit-up institutional occupancy building. In fact, the parallel track process of planning and shell construction coupled with team organization are two innovations that few health care facilities have ever attempted for this kind of design and construction."

This kind of forward thinking and pioneering design, planning, and construction are all in a day's work for the principals and professionals of Ellerbe Becket, Inc.

Above: Ellerbe Becket, Inc. designed the Gonda Building, the 1.5 million-square-foot centerpiece of the Mayo Clinic's practice integration projects.

TSP

Integrating architecture, interior design, engineering, and construction services, this single-source Rochester firm with offices throughout the Midwest meets design challenges with innovative solutions based on teamwork, client collaboration, and attention to detail.

Above: TSP teamed with the community on the expansion and remodeling of both the Mayo Civic Center and the Rochester Civic Theatre.

TSP, a single-source architecture firm, is uniquely positioned to blend functionality with artistic appeal. This Rochester firm's comprehensive architectural, engineering, interior design, and construction services provide creative solutions that achieve clients' goals.

Art and Architecture

Architect Harold Spitznagel founded TSP more than 75 years ago in Sioux Falls, South Dakota. Today the firm continues to build art into architecture, echoing the founder's belief in creative design and innovation.

TSP follows a simple precept of collaboration: "To Solve. To Excel. Together." With seven offices throughout the Midwest, TSP draws on the knowledge and expertise of its professionals while incorporating client feedback; it believes that success hinges on listening to the client. The results of such collaboration consistently top client expectations.

Integrated Services

The close working relationship of TSP teams throughout the region means holistic, integrated approaches to designing buildings.

Knowing that one size does not fit all, TSP begins each project with a clear understanding of the client's specific needs, challenges, budget, and schedule. The professionals at TSP recognize that working together helps them create better buildings. TSP engineers—civil, electrical, mechanical, and structural—work closely with architects and contractors to achieve the company's signature fusion of art and functionality. The construction team manages cost efficiency and quality.

Distinctive Design, Impressive Results

TSP's portfolio testifies to the success of its approach; the firm has designed and built thousands of properties nationwide in the health care, education, recreation, senior living, and public sectors.

Notably, TSP helped expand and remodel the Mayo Civic Center and Rochester Recreation Center. TSP architects and engineers also have been pivotal in projects for the Rochester Park and Recreation Department, Olmsted County, Rochester Public Works, Rochester Civic Theatre, Rochester Area Family Y, Samaritan Bethany, Quarry Hill Nature Center, Soldier Field Bathhouse, and Rochester Community and Technical College.

Community Support and Inspiration

As an active firm in the community, TSP is involved in many civic and charitable organizations. Whether through architecture or community service, TSP inspires and adds value to Rochester.

Quality craftsmanship, innovative design, and proven expertise define this longtime Rochester home builder, remodeler, and maintenance firm. Using the highest design and construction standards, it brings each client's vision to life. The company's work reflects its appreciation of elegant living.

Summit has set the standard in elite custom-designed home building by developing singular and sophisticated solutions to client requests. It understands the complex dance of blending an owner's vision with the design-build process—and it knows the steps well. Its thoughtful and proven approach integrates the neighborhood, lot, view, and style of the home in order to maximize the owner's investment. Summit is acclaimed for creating fresh, striking living environments that combine beauty, simplicity, and integrity.

Summit's success springs from its talented leadership and staff. Partners and master carpenters Jack Gabor and Monte Viker work closely with each client to deliver creativity and accountability. Project director Janet Wagner handles all budget and project management details. And all of the company's full-time employees carry out their work with expertise and efficiency. Summit's uncompromising standards exceed building codes and apply to every aspect of both new and remodeled homes.

A company's work reflects its values. Each Summit creation is designed to embody elegance and beauty from the roof down to the smallest finished details. It steps beyond traditional interior design by collaborating with Kenna Sanborn of Design Forte, LLC to work directly with clients to provide creative consulting and implementation through every step of the design-build process. This practice is followed to ensure that only the finest materials and techniques are used, and that the result is seamless style and uncommon ambience, comfort, and livability that lend a natural harmony to daily life.

To help busy clients find the time to enjoy their fine homes, Summit offers LifeStyle, a maintenance service that works to protect the owner's real estate investment. Services include comprehensive home inspections, post-inspection reports and recommendations, monthly service plans, house supervision when owners travel, and on-demand service calls.

Summit's work reflects its love of the elegant lifestyle and its philosophy of excellence and complete customer satisfaction.

Above, all photos: Summit Custom Homes has designed, built, and remodeled some of southeastern Minnesota's finest homes for more than 25 years. Inside and out, every Summit creation has its own unique appeal, and the company strives to ensure that each one fits harmoniously into its environment.

Weis Builders, Inc.

From a simple cabinetmaking operation in the founder's basement to one of the top contractors in the country, this versatile, family-owned business has a presence in national construction markets. Virtually all major businesses in Rochester have put their trust and confidence in Weis Builders over the years.

Both photos: The four-story, 83-key Staybridge Suites in Rochester (above) and the 136,933-square-foot Lowe's hardware store (right) are among the many notable new-construction projects recently completed by Weis Builders, Inc.

In 1939 John Weis started a cabinet shop in the basement of his home in Rochester. His reputation for quality workmanship spread, and soon he was offering remodeling services and custom-designed home construction.

His sons, Eugene and Joseph (Joe), worked with their father from childhood, learning his carpentry and business skills. Eugene joined the family business (called John Weis & Sons at the time) in 1946 upon returning from military service. Joe soon followed after completing a course in architectural drafting

and estimating at Dunwoody Industrial Institute in Minneapolis.

When John Weis passed away in 1952, Eugene and Joe carried on the family tradition. Their first independent job was a simple garage. For a time, they continued to be primarily residential and commercial remodelers, but their ambition brought them to the threshold of larger things. In 1960 they incorporated the business under the name Weis Builders, Inc. and soon began constructing commercial and light industrial buildings.

Today the third generation of the Weis family has earned a leadership role in the business. And members of the fourth generation are learning the business as project managers and estimators.

From the beginning, Weis Builders has been known for its versatility. The company is involved in various markets, including multifamily residential, health care, senior living, retail, hospitality, commercial, and industrial construction. The work ranges in size from small remodeling jobs to major new construction.

From the Olmsted County Recreation Center, Rochester Towers, and Michaels Restaurant to GrandeVille at Cascade Lake, the Zumbro Valley Mental Health Center campus, and the University of Minnesota Rochester at University Square, Weis Builders has been influential in shaping the built environment in Rochester. It has also been a preferred contractor for Mayo Clinic and for IBM since the mid 1980s.

The company's Rochester office delivers the advantages of a small-town contractor while bringing the perspective and financial clout of a company that conducts business on a national level. Weis Builders also serves clients from its offices in Minneapolis, Minnesota, and in Chicago, Illinois. The company

provides additional information on its Web site (www.weisbuilders.com).

The company earns and retains the trust and confidence of the clients it serves. Jamey Shandley, vice president of Hamilton Real Estate, Inc., a long-time client, states, "We have had the opportunity to work with Weis Builders on a number of projects through the years. We have always been impressed with the manner in which Weis Builders has communicated with us during each construction project. Every project has been completed on time with outstanding quality."

The Weis Builders reputation for dependability and craftsmanship accounts for its large volume of repeat business with a wide range of clients.

The Hexum Companies

This full-service retail, office, and industrial real estate development company—which originated from R. L. Hexum and Associates, Inc. and R. L. Hexum Builders, Inc.—has helped shape the Rochester community and skyline. In so doing, it has also helped shape the great quality of life and work in its hometown.

The Hexum Companies team of professionals provides clients with quality services through a streamlined, efficient process—from inception to completion.

As market and societal trends shift, so does the need for diversifying real estate services and development. The Hexum Companies' core knowledge of the land development business combined with its real estate brokerage base has provided the Rochester community with unique, innovative, and lasting projects. The success of this company's collaboration with quality local firms and partners over the past five decades has resulted in such notable projects as the Baihly Woodlands, Green Meadows, Glendale, and Woodgate communities.

Photo: © Bordner Aerials

Shoppes on Maine

In 2007 the emphasis for the Hexum Companies was on its involvement with Maine Street Development and with Opus NW LLC in creating and marketing the Shoppes on Maine/Canal Place Retail Development, located at the south entrance to Rochester.

Shoppes on Maine is the retail component of a master-planned, 500-acre mixed-use development. When complete, the retail segment will exceed 1.5 million square feet. Its Power Center is anchored by Dick's Sporting Goods, Lowe's, Mills Fleet Farm, Target, Toyota, and Wehrenberg Theatres.

At Shoppes on Maine, waterfalls, walking paths to neighboring residential developments, and lush parkland are designed to come together in a work-residential-entertainment environment that is within easy walking distance or short driving distance for residents.

The Canal Place segment, which complements Shoppes on Maine, features dining venues, theaters, boutiques, coffee shops, and banking facilities. This total project will provide a convenient place for residents and visitors to shop and gather.

Community and Family

The Hexum Companies' core belief has always been that its community and the families who live there make Rochester the great city that it is. Every year the owners of the Hexum Companies give back in service, time, scholarships, and sponsorships to the residents of Rochester, the University of Minnesota Rochester, the Rochester Community and Technical College, and affordable-housing organizations. Beginning in 2007, the new Lourdes High School will be the primary focus of the Hexum Companies.

With the company experiencing double-digit growth, the Hexum Companies sees bright days ahead based on its ability to diversify, to meet market trends, and to give back to the community. Rochester is Minnesota's fastest-growing city, a trend attributed to its business community's commitment to residents and visitors alike.

The Hexum Companies is proud to be a part of this tradition and commitment.

Left: Shown in 2007, construction is under way for the Shoppes on Maine/Canal Place Retail Development, a 500-acre mixed-use site located at the south entrance to Rochester.

After losing his life savings in the Great Depression, Andrew Chafoulias decided to make a fresh start in a new city. Coming to Rochester turned out to be a smart move for Andrew. The Greek immigrant and entrepreneur began several business ventures, including a restaurant called the North Crystal Cafe, a liquor business that his sons still operate, and multiple land investments.

His sons, Gus, James, and Ted, used the business sense they inherited from their father and established Chafoulias Companies, also known as Chafoulias Management Company (CMC), in 1977. Over the past 30 years, the family-owned company has developed more than three million square feet of commercial real estate and over 2,000 apartment units, becoming one of the city's most successful real estate developers and one of its highest tax payers.

CMC owns and operates three hotels in Rochester: the Radisson Plaza Hotel, the Hilton Garden Inn, and Sleep Inn and Suites near Rochester International Airport. CMC manages the U.S. Bank office tower on First Avenue and the Galleria Mall shopping center as well.

CMC is not the only business venture owned and operated by the Chafoulias family. James Chafoulias owns Pioneer Paper Co., which has factories in Minneapolis, Kansas City, Dallas, and Chicago. Ted Chafoulias owns K&M Glass, along with numerous real estate investments. Ted's sons, Mark and Chris, own several Slumberland stores. Gus's son, Andrew, owns Global Resolve and Rochester Yellow Cab with his cousins, Mark and Chris. In addition, Andrew has founded several companies and has headed many developments, including the expansion of Rochester International Airport. Andrew pioneered development at the airport as his father helped pioneer the development of downtown Rochester.

Another Chafoulias-owned business in Rochester, Andy's Liquor Inc., a retailer and distributor of wine and spirits started by Andrew Chafoulias in 1934, was originally located down-town. Andrew's sons, who moved the business to the Crossroads Shopping Center in 1963, operate the company today. A popular local store, Andy's Liquor offers a monthly wine newsletter, wine tasting, and party planning.

The Chafoulias family takes pride in its heritage and its strong ties to the community. Gus remembers growing up in Rochester when just a handful of Greek families lived among the town's 18,000 people. His feelings of being different inspired him to help other immigrants in Rochester gain economic and social parity. As one of Rochester's influential business-men, he served on the board of

Building Equality Together, an organization to fight racism and discrimination, and helped with its fund-raising. In 1995 this organization became the Diversity Council, which the family still supports through personal memberships and donations from the Chafoulias Companies.

The Chafoulias family has a lot to be proud of, as its first, second, and third generations have all worked very hard and are each successful in their own ways. The family members also manage to maintain very close relationships with each other.

Yaggy Colby Associates

Formed in 1970, this multidisciplinary consulting firm has built its success on the creativity of individual ideas reinforced through communication, teamwork, and quality services that meet every client's needs.

The professionals at Yaggy Colby Associates have extensive experience in the master planning, design, and implementation of a range of projects, from single-family subdivisions to office and industrial parks to shopping centers. The firm's clients within the building and site design, municipal, transportation, and land development service areas depend on Yaggy Colby Associates for well-focused, comprehensive solutions; prompt, personal assistance; and a full array of design services. The firm's integrated multidisciplinary approach incorporates engineering, architecture, landscape architecture, surveying, and planning.

Yaggy Colby Associates' engineering expertise encompasses city engineering services; the design of municipal infrastructure items, including water systems, sanitary sewer systems, lift stations, parking lots, and ramps; residential, industrial, and planned-unit site developments; the design of transportation facilities, including roads, streets, highways, interchanges, bridges, traffic signals, airports, and railroads; and structural, environmental, and geotechnical engineering.

Yaggy Colby Associates' architecture expertise extends to shopping malls, bank and office buildings, schools, libraries, churches, condominium and townhome developments, multifamily residential units, park and public buildings, and historic preservation and restoration.

The firm's focus on landscape architecture includes master plans; streetscapes and plazas; residential, commercial, and industrial developments; wetland delineation; wetland mitigation plans and permits; planned-unit developments; park improvements; athletic fields; tennis courts; playgrounds; biking and hiking trails; and land use, zoning, and site-analysis services.

In surveying, Yaggy Colby Associates covers boundary, topography, subdivision plans, hydrography, construction, highway and route sites, remonumentation, easements, horizontal and vertical control networks, photogrammetric control, and more.

In the area of planning, Yaggy Colby Associates facilitates community projects, including comprehensive, strategic, and economic development plans; transportation planning; grant applications and administration; downtown revitalization; housing rehabilitation; zoning and subdivision ordinances; tax increment financing; commercial and industrial development; capital improvement; and community design analysis.

Among this firm's outstanding contributions to the Rochester area are residential neighborhoods such as Century Hills, Northern Hills, and Stone Hedge, plus numerous southwest developments around the Folwell and Baihly farms. Yaggy Colby Associates was also part of the national award–winning ROC 52 Highway Project design team, and the firm has designed numerous public improvements and water towers throughout the community. Yaggy Colby Associates' landscape architects have designed several local parks and plazas, including Chester Woods Regional Park and the recent First Street Plaza in downtown Rochester. Commercial developments of note include a remodel and expansion at the Apache Mall Regional Shopping Center, the Northwest Plaza, Rochester Public Library, Rochester Fire Stations Numbers Three and Five, and the recent Shoppes on Maine development.

All photos: These images represent the municipal, transportation, building and site design, and land development services that Yaggy Colby Associates has provided to its public and private clients for more than 36 years. Pictured above, clockwise from top left, are the Century Hills Development, Mayo Plaza, the ROC 52 Highway Project, Apache Mall, and Merchant's Bank. Yaggy Colby Associates' corporate office is proudly located in Rochester, with regional offices in Minneapolis–St. Paul, Minnesota; Milwaukee, Wisconsin; and Mason City, Iowa.

Johnson Controls, Inc.

Founded in 1885 with a patent that launched the building control industry, this company is a global leader in products for automotive interiors, power solutions, and building efficiency. It has continued its bold course of technological innovation and expertise toward enabling a more comfortable, safe, and sustainable world.

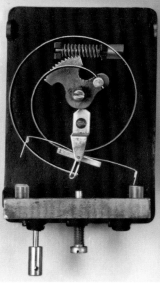

Above: Three of the earliest endeavors of Johnson Controls, Inc. were this radio tower in Cudahy, Wisconsin—thought to be the first wireless telegraph tower west of the Atlantic Coast; this 1907 "auto carriage;" and this giant floral clock for the 1904 World's Fair in St. Louis. Above center: The "electric telethermostat," the first electric thermostat for a room, was invented by Warren S. Johnson in 1883. Above right: Johnson founded Johnson Controls in 1885.

In 1883, Warren S. Johnson, a professor at the State Normal School in Whitewater, Wisconsin, was awarded a patent for the first electric room thermostat. In 1885, with patent in hand, Johnson went on to form Johnson Controls, Inc. to manufacture, install, and provide service for automatic temperature regulation systems for buildings.

A Century of Growth

Today, 100-plus years later, Johnson Controls has grown to encompass 140,000 employees in more than 1,000 locations and to serve customers in 170 countries worldwide. While Johnson Controls has remained in the technological forefront of the controls industry, this Milwaukee, Wisconsin–based company also has evolved into a global leader in other areas such as automotive interiors and power solutions. In fact, it is one of the world's largest manufacturers of lead-acid automotive batteries and a developer of advanced battery chemistries. It also manufactures batteries for hybrid electric vehicles as well as emergency power backup and telecommunications applications.

True to Its Roots

Through more than a century of growth and expansion, Johnson Controls continues to excel in its original area of expertise—building efficiency. The company has built its reputation on automating, integrating, and increasing the efficiency of critical building systems, such as heating, ventilating, and air-conditioning (HVAC); lighting; security; and fire safety. From the beginning, Johnson Controls focused on increasing a building's energy efficiency and operational performance. Today, the company provides mechanical equipment as well as systems for commercial, institutional, and industrial facilities.

With more than 500 locations worldwide devoted to the company's Johnson Controls Building Efficiency business, Johnson Controls opened its first Rochester office in 1991. Today, this Rochester branch is devoted entirely to building efficiency, including systems, service, and solutions.

Investing in Its Communities

The success of Johnson Controls in Rochester and worldwide is largely attributed to the company's commitment to excellence and quality. However, it also reflects the company's commitment to its local communities. Johnson Controls responds to local and international communities through generous philanthropic support and volunteer activities. For example, in 2006 the company donated a training laboratory for digital building automation to the Rochester Community and Technical College. Johnson Controls also contributes to Hiawatha Homes for the physically challenged through Rochester's annual Festival of Trees.

Kendall Roche, branch manager of the Johnson Controls Rochester branch, notes, "In 2006, Johnson Controls took a giant leap forward when we signed a performance contract with the city—for everything from street lights to the Rochester Civic Center and all city-owned property. We are energy solution partners with Rochester Public Utilities, providing energy management systems to make our city a role model in energy savings."

From its key role in the construction of Mayo Clinic's Gonda Building to the building of schools, religious institutions, banks, parking ramps, health care facilities, and City Hall in Rochester, Knutson Construction Services, based in Minneapolis, has become one of Rochester's most respected contractors.

After 40 years of managing Rochester construction projects through its Minneapolis Office, Knutson extended its commitment to the city in 1997, opening an office in Rochester. Celebrating its 10th anniversary in Rochester in 2007, the company opened a large new office off Highway 52—one large enough to accommodate its outstanding associates, who serve as a model for the entire organization.

Knutson focuses on the community and cares deeply about Rochester's growth and the people who live there. "It is very rewarding for all of us to look at the skyline and know that Knutson has played a large part in helping to create this great community," says David Bastyr, vice president and general manager of the Rochester division.

The company's dedication to understanding customer needs has set industry standards for service and quality, earning Knutson the trust and respect of many organizations integral to the city. For example, the *Rochester Post-Bulletin*, which occupies a 50-year-old building, turns to Knutson for major construction work and ongoing projects. When the local newspaper's air conditioner failed on the hottest day of 2006, Knutson swiftly responded and replaced the 900-pound rooftop air-conditioning unit—in hours, not days. Knutson's dedicated employees, along with those of Hawk & Sons, TEC Industrial, and Ryan Electric, allowed the newspaper to keep the presses running.

Knutson also more than doubled the number of rooms, from 29 to 61, at the American Cancer Society's Hope Lodge, where cancer patients and their families receive free housing. Knutson not only minimized inconvenience to guests during construction but also facilitated many in-kind contributions from subcontractors and suppliers to save significant funds for this important Rochester organization.

Knutson considers its business to be about more than hammering nails and pouring concrete; it is about building a community, contributing to society, and turning ideas into lasting structures. It is about a team of professionals who are passionate, competent, innovative, and proud to help clients transform their dreams into reality.

Left: Knutson Construction Services has played a key role in the construction of Rochester's City Hall (shown here) as well as the Mayo Clinic's Gonda Building; area schools, religious institutions, banks, and health care facilities; and much more. Knutson has earned its position and reputation as one of Rochester's most respected contractors.

Hammel, Green and Abrahamson, Inc.

For more than 50 years, this architectural, engineering, and interior design firm has helped to shape the environments of culture, commerce, and society by creating innovative, enduring spaces for its clients and communities.

Founded in 1953, Hammel, Green and Abrahamson, Inc. (HGA) is a full-service architecture, engineering, and interior design firm. Organized into interdisciplinary practice groups, HGA offers a balanced portfolio of planning and design expertise with a focus on corporate, health care, arts, community and education, and science and technology. Nationally recognized and award-winning, HGA creates lasting, environmentally intelligent designs nationwide.

With offices in Rochester and Minneapolis, Minnesota; Milwaukee, Wisconsin; and Sacramento, San Francisco, and Los Angeles, California, the firm addresses each project with an interdisciplinary, collaborative, and client-focused approach.

Beyond Bricks and Mortar

HGA helps clients meet their specific needs and realize their vision. A team approaches a project through the client's eyes to fully understand all project requirements and budget needs. Then the team translates the client's vision into practical solutions—considering aesthetics, usefulness, safety, accessibility, costs, and return on investment. The goal is a cost-effective, innovative, and functional design.

Through this process, HGA also embraces the concept of sustainable design—smart growth, environmental sensitivity, and a commitment to meet current needs without compromising the interests of future generations. Using sustainable design, HGA balances the impact of development with ecological and environmental respect. The result is a building with higher energy efficiency, lower operating costs, and aesthetic harmony with the environment.

Buildings That Touch Lives

For over half a century, HGA evolved into one of the most innovative design firms, first in the Midwest and then nationally. The firm has shaped environments for corporate clients, the health care industry, religious groups, museums, schools, and more. HGA's vast portfolio of buildings has touched people's lives and enhanced their environment. Regardless of the project or its location, HGA brings a high level of expertise while retaining a local presence with an intimate, personal approach.

HGA looks to the future with the same commitment to design excellence upon which it has built its reputation over its more than 50 years. HGA principal Hal Henderson reflects, "Our clients' goals, objectives, business challenges, and expectations come first. Every project is a unique opportunity. The architect must link the imagination with the opportunities of each project. Anything can be done, but achieving our clients' goals within the limitations they establish is true success. We are responsible for being both a motivator and an innovator."

Bigelow Homes

With more than 30 years of construction, home-building, and development experience in southeastern Minnesota, this small, highly successful company has earned a reputation for customer satisfaction by building quality houses that make the most out of each dollar spent.

Above: The experienced team at Bigelow Homes includes, from left to right: Jordan Barnes, project manager; Matt Simon, assistant vice president and project manager; Denel Ihde, director of sales and marketing; Mike Paradise, president; and Jeremy Bigelow, vice president and project manager.

Ten Reasons to Build with Bigelow Homes

1. Bigelow excels in all types of houses, from townhomes to custom-designed homes.
2. Bigelow's comprehensive Web site (www.bigelowhomes.net) guides customers through the home-building process.
3. The company has built homes in southeastern Minnesota for over 30 years.
4. Bigelow works with the same trusted, experienced subcontractors on each job.
5. A seamless-service team stays with customers from start to finish.
6. A full-time service department is always available.
7. Customers can personalize their homes with a choice of modern decor.
8. Customers can choose from hundreds of lots in 10 southeastern Minnesota communities.
9. Unlimited options in floor plans will fit any customer's needs.
10. Bigelow Homes will be in the community for years to come.

As a young man, Joel Bigelow worked in construction until he decided to work for himself. At the age of 20, he began fixing roofs and shingling homes and barns with his own crew. The fledgling company then started constructing commercial buildings. Joel eventually built a home for his family, at which point he saw the huge potential in building cost-efficient single-family homes.

Today Bigelow Homes grosses more than $50 million per year in sales, building houses in Austin, Byron, Dodge Center, Kasson, Kellogg, Kenyon, Mantorville, Pine Island, Rochester, and Zumbrota, Minnesota. Bigelow considers his organization to be aggressive but also hardworking and honest. "I never dreamed that our company would be this large," he says. "My vision has always been to do the best job possible for the least cost and to be honest and ethical with our customers." Bigelow Homes subcontracts a good part of its work, and it has 35 people on staff—including managers, job coordinators, carpenters, and repairmen who provide service for homes built by the company.

When choosing property to develop, Bigelow Homes anticipates the needs of the residential real estate market and the locales where people tend to be going. Bigelow acknowledges the role of luck but considers it the intersection of preparation and opportunity. The company also believes that positive people and companies get more business. "Bigelow Homes treats everyone, from maintenance workers to painters to bank presidents, with the same respect," he says. "We are thankful to be part of the growing community of Rochester."

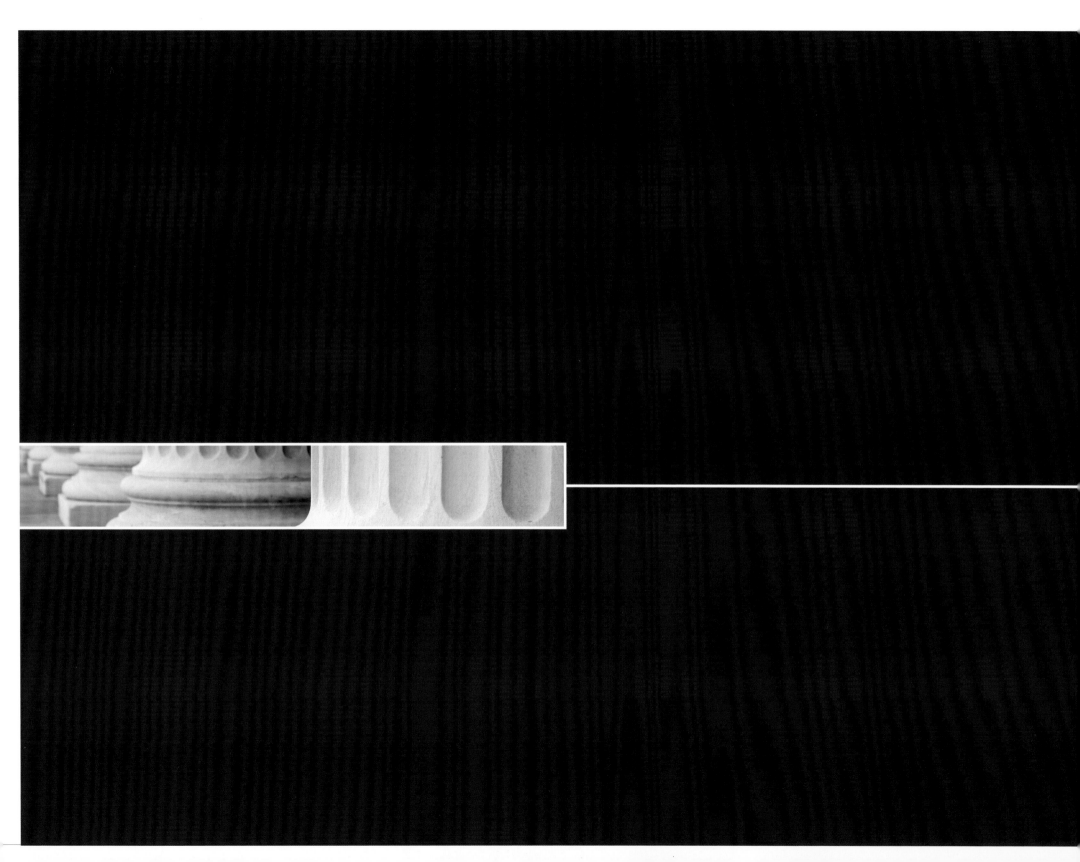

PROFILES OF COMPANIES AND ORGANIZATIONS

Civic and Cultural Enhancement and Religious Services

Rochester Area Foundation

This community foundation improves the quality of life, promotes greater equality of opportunities, and develops effective methods to assist those in need in the greater Rochester area. Through grant making and proactive leadership, it strengthens community philanthropy and helps donors meet their charitable objectives.

Rochester
Area Foundation

Above: The Rochester Area Foundation's logo was adopted for its 60th anniversary in 2004. The tree represents the foundation's past growth and its bright future. Right: Happy homeowners stand outside their newly purchased home, which was made possible through First Homes and its community land trust and Heritage Homes programs.

In 1942, Harry J. Harwick had no idea what his quiet community would look like more than 60 years later, but he knew he wanted to be part of it. The longtime Mayo Foundation chairman envisioned an organization that would grow, sustain, and better his community for generations. His desire to give back took shape two years later in 1944, in the form of the Rochester Community Foundation, today called the Rochester Area Foundation.

Enduring Legacies

Since it began, the Rochester Area Foundation has existed to serve its donors and provide the community with a collective endowment for all time. The individuals, families, and corporations that invest in the foundation play an active and meaningful role in their community because their gifts continue giving for generations, making a difference over and over again. Thanks to the strong, adept leadership of its board of trustees—composed today, as in the past, of prominent community leaders—the Rochester Area Foundation invests wisely to ensure the perpetuity of its assets and thereby the ongoing strength of the community.

Grants and Growth

One of the most significant ways the foundation helps donors meet their charitable objectives is through grant making. The foundation's tradition of giving has driven much of the positive change and growth in its community. Made possible by gifts from generous donors, grant awards target significant needs, emerging challenges, and opportunities for increased economic vitality and quality of life. Through this work, the Rochester Area Foundation demonstrates the transformative power of philanthropy. This power, coupled with a compelling community vision, allows the foundation to help the community attain its aspirations.

FAMILY LITERACY VAN

Transforming Greater Rochester

In recent years, the foundation has branched out to include two community development initiatives, widening the scope of its proactive, transformational leadership. It created First Homes in 1999 to address a communitywide housing shortage. In the years since, First Homes has employed strategies to make home ownership a reality for hundreds of working families across Greater Rochester. By incorporating a community land trust (CLT) framework, for example, the program allows

qualified homebuyers to purchase a home for tens of thousands of dollars less than market value. These properties remain in the CLT forever, ensuring future homebuyers the same reasonably priced housing opportunities.

First Homes offers a unique mix of housing options by working with both new and existing construction. Through its Heritage Homes program, First Homes reinvests in Rochester's oldest, core neighborhoods by rehabilitating and restoring old homes that have fallen into disrepair.

These houses are then put back on the market as part of the CLT.

First Homes also revitalizes these neighborhoods by helping residents establish comprehensive "vision" plans. These efforts significantly improve the livability and economic vitality of the core neighborhoods.

Ensuring the Success of Future Generations

Rochester Area Foundation's second initiative, First Steps, began in 2005 to ensure that all children have the chance to develop intellectually, socially, and emotionally. As an alarming number of Rochester-area children enter school unready to learn, First Steps serves as a convener to prepare every child for success in school. Community collaborators have made great strides toward this goal. Hundreds of child care providers, educators, and parents have completed SEEDS of Early Literacy training; numerous children have been removed from a waiting list and given scholarships to attend high quality preschool; and there has been a dramatic increase in the number of

parents bringing their children for kindergarten readiness check-ins at age three to detect potential problems early.

Continuing the Tradition

As the Rochester Area Foundation looks to the future, many of its core goals and principles remain the same: provide an effective outlet for giving, catalyze positive change, and carefully manage the contributions of its philanthropic partners, ensuring that each gift continues giving in perpetuity. The foundation also anticipates launching other community development initiatives to continue its tradition of responding to unmet community needs.

Though Harry J. Harwick did not live to see his brainchild mature into the organization it is today, his vision survives through the strength and careful guidance of the foundation's board of trustees. These dedicated individuals, along with each foundation contributor, ensure that the same spirit of philanthropy and leadership that sparked Rochester Area Foundation's inception will live on forever.

cf NATIONAL STANDARDS℠

Left: K-Ready—the kangaroo mascot of the Rochester Area Foundation's First Steps early-childhood education initiative—visits Rochester children at a summer literacy program. First Steps partners with many community organizations to ensure that all children are ready to learn when they enter kindergarten. Above: After completing a rigorous peer review, the Rochester Area Foundation was awarded the Council on Foundations seal of approval, which signifies that it meets national standards for excellence and accountability.

City of Rochester

This unique, contemporary city—an area of opportunity for commercial and industrial development, business expansion, and entrepreneurial ventures—combines a cosmopolitan atmosphere with small-town friendliness for a high quality of life and serves as an economic growth center and cultural hub for southern Minnesota.

Above left: Graced with natural and man-made amenities, the City of Rochester offers many opportunities for outdoor activities, such as world-class golfing, as well as swimming and tennis, ice-skating and cross-country skiing. Above right: This panoramic view speaks to *Money* magazine's description of Rochester as "radiating cosmopolitan style without big city ills."

The third-largest city in the state of Minnesota and one of the state's fastest-growing municipalities, the City of Rochester has frequently been listed among the best places to live by *Money* magazine, ranking 67th in 2006.

The mention of Minnesota can conjure up images of cold weather, towering snow banks, and small rural towns; however, Rochester contradicts such impressions. While winter temperatures dip to an average low of three degrees, Rochester enjoys an average of 200 sunny days annually. And the city's

strong economy, built on a foundation of agricultural enterprise, also is fueled by the health care, high-technology, and hospitality industries.

Located in Olmsted County in southeastern Minnesota, Rochester has been described by *Money* as "radiating cosmopolitan style without big city ills."

Strong, Viable Economy

Its high quality of life, stable economy, and worker productivity make Rochester a desirable place in which to live. Its local economy remains stable

throughout national economic ups and downs. In fact, its economy continues to grow at a pace that exceeds that of not only the rest of the state but also the entire nation.

Rochester's economy is driven by a variety of development incentives from state and local sources. One such source, Rochester Area Economic Development, Inc. (RAEDI) works to facilitate the growth of businesses in Rochester. RAEDI helps qualifying enterprises secure the resources needed for development, start-up,

expansion, or relocation to the area. One example of its many projects is its support for Rochester's new bioscience facility, the Minnesota BioBusiness Center, projected for completion in 2008.

Rochester is perhaps best known for its two largest employers: Mayo Clinic and IBM. Founded in 1914, Mayo Clinic, one of the nation's leading destinations for patient care and medical research, is the largest employer in Rochester and one of the largest in the state. It employs more than 28,000 people locally and indirectly supports an additional 40,000 jobs in Minnesota. IBM is the second-largest local employer. Its 3.6 million-square-foot complex, the world's largest IBM facility under one roof, has some 4,400 workers. With the development and manufacturing of IBM's super-computer Blue Gene/L, employment is projected to increase. Numerous other high-tech companies in Rochester produce computer hardware and software.

Agribusiness is the area's third-largest industry. Olmsted County is home to some 1,400 working farms, which account for 60 percent of land use. Food processors include vegetable

packers, and there are three large dairy processors and a cannery. Rochester also is home to an extensive service industry, which accounts for more than 80 percent of jobs in the area. The city's hospitality companies serve some 1.5 million visitors per year, and the area is a regional center for shoppers.

Emphasis on Education

Rochester puts a premium on providing education that begins with early childhood. In fact, since 1974 the city has had a voluntary public school program for early childhood family education, called Parents Are Important In Rochester (PAIIR).

Beyond offering early childhood education, the Rochester area has six separate school districts, with nearly 23,000 students enrolled in public elementary and secondary schools. Private schools in Rochester have a combined enrollment of close to 3,000 students. Rochester students regularly score above state and national averages. Perhaps more significantly, more than 85 percent of graduating high school seniors pursue postsecondary education.

Higher education in Rochester is an important factor in the quality of life and economic vitality of southeastern Minnesota. Several higher education institutions serve the region, providing undergraduate, graduate, and workforce education programs in business, education, health sciences, technology, and liberal arts. The University of Minnesota Rochester, which is located in downtown Rochester near Mayo Clinic, focuses on academic programs and research in the biosciences and biotechnology. Rochester Community and Technical College and Winona State University–Rochester offer "one-stop shopping" for students at the University Center Rochester, a partnership of higher education campuses.

Recreation and Entertainment

Rochester offers much in the way of entertainment and recreation. In 2004 the Rochester Art Center was opened adjacent to Mayo Park and downtown Rochester. The bold, 36,000-square-foot facility, which edges the Zumbro

River, consists of two architectural volumes—one copper, one zinc—linked by a glass-framed grand lobby. The city also is home to a number of theaters including the Rochester Civic Theatre, the Masque Youth Theatre, and the Rochester Repertory Theatre, as well as various musical ensembles and orchestras.

Additionally, Rochester offers many opportunities to enjoy outdoor activities. The city has an expansive park system with more than 100 sites covering five square miles, as well as more than 60 miles of city trails for running, hiking, and biking. Other local activities include golf, swimming, and tennis, and in the winter, ice-skating and cross-country skiing. Local team sports include hockey, football, and baseball.

On the Move

Rochester counters its months of winter temperatures by interconnecting its downtown area with one of

the most extensive subway-skyway systems in the nation for a city of its size. Climate-controlled skyways and underground walkways are designed to ensure that downtown businesses, hotels, stores, and restaurants all can be accessed without pedestrians having to step outside.

Living Up to Its Reputation

The Rochester Area Chamber of Commerce once described Rochester as "the economic growth center and cultural hub of southern Minnesota." The city's productive and efficient labor force, world-renowned medical facilities, excellent educational system, and high quality of life are some of the reasons why Rochester is considered to be one of the best places to live in the United States.

Above left: A Rochester landmark, Mayowood Estate was created by Mayo Clinic cofounder Dr. Charles H. Mayo between 1911 and 1938. The estate, with Mayowood Mansion and surrounding gardens, is operated by the Olmsted County Historical Society as a historic house museum. Above right: The Soldiers Field Veterans Memorial, located in Rochester, was created to honor the military veterans from southeast Minnesota who died serving the United States and is dedicated to all the men and women who have served the nation.

The Franciscan Sisters of Rochester

One of the world's largest private hospitals—Saint Marys Hospital in Rochester—was founded more than 100 years ago by this benevolent religious order. Organized in 1877, the Franciscan Sisters of Rochester have made great strides in health, education, and social justice, not only at home but also abroad.

The Franciscan Sisters of Rochester believe that God is all-present—in suffering, in need, in beauty, even in a summer storm's violence.

The tornado that ripped through Rochester in August 1883 led to Saint Marys Hospital. In the aftermath of the storm, Mother Alfred Moes, founder of the Rochester Franciscans, approached Dr. William Worrall Mayo with a proposal: the sisters would build a hospital if he and his sons, Drs. Will and Charlie, would staff it. Today, Saint Marys is one of the largest private hospitals in the world, and in 1986 the hospital became part of the world-famous Mayo Clinic. Through sponsorship, the sisters still affect the daily life of the hospital.

Numbering 290, the Rochester Franciscans have reached out to many states and several foreign countries.

There are also more than 120 Cojourners, people who share the sisters' values and spirituality. The congregational center, Assisi Heights, crowns a Rochester hill and is visible for miles around. It serves not only as the congregation's home but also as an ecumenical center for various churches in the area.

The Rochester Franciscans were primarily teachers of elementary and secondary students in the parochial schools of southern Minnesota and other midwestern states; others were nurses. In 1894 they founded what became the College of Saint Teresa in Winona, Minnesota, for women who would use their education to influence the world. In the 1960s, the sisters expanded their ministry in education and health care to Bogota, Colombia, and began pastoral work in Peru. Cambodians, too, benefit from a school established by the Rochester Franciscans that teaches adults to teach others.

The spirit of Mother Alfred Moes—tireless doer of the Gospel—lives on in her sisters. Today, Rochester Franciscans can be found in many ministries, including education, health care, pastoral care, social services, and peace and justice. Committed to being a compassionate presence for peace in the world, striving for justice and reverence for all creation, the sisters generously share who they are and what they have, and they strive to be faithful to the call of Jesus, the charism of St. Francis and St. Clare, and the vision of Mother Alfred Moes.

Above: Visible for miles around, Assisi Heights is the congregational center of the Franciscan Sisters of Rochester.

Rochester Civic Theatre

Host to award-winning productions and innovative educational and outreach programs that touch the lives of more than 30,000 adults and children each year, this exciting venue offers the local and surrounding communities stellar live theatre performances in a prime downtown location.

A premier theatrical performance venue in southeast Minnesota and one of the state's largest community theatres, Rochester Civic Theatre dates back to 1951, when a group of theatre enthusiasts known as the Log Cabin Players made plans to "put on a show." The performers each contributed $10 of their own money to produce Moss Hart's *Light Up the Sky*. Inspired by the production's success, the troupe became formally incorporated, initially producing a three-show season.

A decade later, a successful capital campaign resulted in a permanent home for the theatre and a new 300-seat facility in a prime downtown location for the Rochester community. In 2001 enhancements to the theatre included an expanded lobby, new classroom space, an updated costume shop, and additional backstage storage. More than half a century after that initial meeting of local performers, the thriving Rochester Civic Theatre, with a focus on flexible performing space and additional instructional areas, is an integral part of downtown development plans.

Governed by a volunteer board of directors and staffed by professional personnel, the award-winning Rochester Civic Theatre maintains a commitment to the high artistic caliber that its audiences have grown to expect—fresh, exciting, and dynamic interpretations of classic and standard theatre fare, as well as new and cutting-edge material. More than 400 local and regional volunteers actively participate each season to support the theatre's year-round slate of productions and its educational and outreach programming. Creative opportunities abound for guest designers, directors, and choreographers from the region to hone and enhance their artistic skills in a professional environment. Theatre resources are readily available to other arts organizations and to the novice as well as the professional performer.

Rochester Civic Theatre fully recognizes its responsibility not only to provide stage entertainment and artistic expression opportunities but also to take an active role in the quality of life and education of the young people and adults of the community. The theatre offers a thriving educational program that includes theatre-based classes, touring troupes, and Summer Theatre Institute, a popular performing camp. In addition, Rochester Civic Theatre houses one of the nation's longest continuously running programs about sexual abuse awareness and prevention. The theatre collaborates with Victim Services and Rochester Public Schools to present performances of "Touch" and "No Easy Answers" each year to area students, educators, and parents.

As a community leader in addressing the importance of diversity in the arts, Rochester Civic Theatre regularly partners with other organizations and businesses to ensure that the arts provide a welcoming environment to foster participation in creative activities.

Above, both photos: Rochester Civic Theatre brings world-class performances—such as the popular musical *Singin' in the Rain* (left) and the stage adaptation of Stephen King's chilling novel *Misery* (right)— to Rochester and the surrounding communities.

PROFILES OF COMPANIES AND ORGANIZATIONS

Education

Rochester Public Schools

From a one-room schoolhouse in 1856 to 22 elementary, middle, and high schools in 2006, Rochester Public Schools and its 16,000 students are the pride of the community. The district's outstanding level of student achievement consistently surpasses both state and national standards.

Above left: Students assemble outside the Phelps School, one of Rochester's first schools, in 1885. The Edison building now occupies the Phelps School site and houses the Rochester Public Schools administrative offices. Above center: Rochester public schools, such as Longfellow 45-15 Choice Elementary School (shown here), educate a diverse range of students. Above right: Eighty-five to 90 percent of the district's graduating seniors move on to higher education.

Rochester Public Schools began in 1856 in one log cabin near the current Riverside Central Elementary School, later moving to a one-room schoolhouse named the Phelps School. Since the 1800s, Rochester has grown significantly, and the district has grown with it. Its program from prekindergarten through grade 12 serves more than 16,000 students in 15 elementary schools, four middle schools, and three high schools. With the seventh-largest enrollment in the state, the district covers a large part of Olmsted County and extends into Wabasha County, drawing from a diverse population of more than 100,000 people.

The third-largest employer in Rochester, the district maintains a staff of about 2,150, including teachers, maintenance workers, clerical staff, student-nutrition staff, administrators, and other support staff. These dedicated employees work together to implement Rochester Public Schools' educational program, which is designed to reach all students, including those with special needs. The district's three strategic aims are High Student Achievement, a Safe and Welcoming Learning Environment, and Efficient and Effective Operations. All goals must support these aims, and every school is expected to have an improvement plan. As a result, student achievement levels consistently top both state and national averages, with 85 to 90 percent of graduating seniors pursuing post–high school education.

The Rochester community has a rich history of showing pride and support for its schools. In 1956, IBM presented a letter to the Rochester School Board stating that an important factor in building an IBM plant in the city was its excellent school system. Today, community members continue to value public education and contribute to student achievement. In 2001, the Rochester community approved a levy to support valuable district programs such as reading intervention, and it renewed that support in 2006.

The district looks to the future with the vision of "Lifelong Learning for All," educating not only elementary- and secondary-school students but also community members. The district's Community Education enrichment program supported this vision by serving 51,741 Rochester residents—including adults, youth, preschool children, and adults with disabilities—during the 2005–06 school year. Rochester's vision today links it to the values of its past, echoing a statement in the 1918 *Report to the Board of Education:* "The responsibility of its public schools is not limited to the traditional courses, but recognizes any activity which makes for better citizenship and more efficient manhood and womanhood."

Founded in 1858 as the first teacher-training institution west of the Mississippi River, Winona State University is built on a powerful sense of place, reflected in distinctive programs and thoughtful engagement with the communities it serves.

With campuses in Rochester and Winona, more than 8,100 students, and 80 undergraduate, graduate, and professional programs, Winona State offers the resources of a major public university. Compact, friendly campuses; small class sizes; close student-faculty interaction; and engagement with the community create an intimate academic environment.

Winona State has served the higher education needs of the Rochester community since 1917. After holding classes in local school buildings for a number of years, the university established one of the first nursing degree programs in the area in response to the community's growing health care industry. Since then, Winona State University–Rochester (WSU–Rochester) has added undergraduate and graduate programs beyond health

science, such as business, education, technology, and the liberal arts.

In 1994 a state-of-the-art campus at University Center Rochester was established through a collaborative agreement between Rochester Community and Technical College and the University of Minnesota. Today students in the region can earn degrees and certificates from associate through doctoral levels in one location.

Students at WSU–Rochester can earn degrees in 12 undergraduate programs and 16 graduate programs. With

access to 40 resident faculty members, convenient day and evening classes, and relationships with IBM Corporation, Mayo Clinic, and Rochester Public Schools, WSU–Rochester students can take advantage of special opportunities and learn skills tailored to the demands of a global economy.

Today more than 5,000 WSU–Rochester alumni live in the Rochester area, teaching children, providing health care for families and friends, exploring the boundaries of technology, and living out the mission of Winona State University.

Throughout its 150-year history, Winona State University has focused on building a model of educational cooperation to meet the emerging intellectual, economic, and social demands of the region. Aligned with the school's motto, "A Community of Learners Dedicated to Improving Our World," WSU–Rochester is in the forefront of the university's mission to prepare leaders who can apply knowledge to find solutions to complex challenges, building a community of lifelong learners who seek to improve the world.

Above right: Winona State University–Rochester students can earn undergraduate and graduate degrees that are tailored to today's global economy. Above left: Goddard Library and Technology Center at University Center Rochester subscribes to more than 13,000 journals and periodicals, and it provides students and faculty with state-of-the-art computing and audiovisual laboratories.

Rochester Community and Technical College

Minnesota's oldest community college offers more than 70 programs and 130 credential opportunities—including health sciences, technology, trade and industry, digital arts, retail and business, and many more—providing a high-caliber faculty and convenient access to a continuum of education.

Above right: Rochester Community and Technical College (RCTC) is located on 518 scenic acres in southeast Rochester. Above left: The main entrance to RCTC—the Atrium—is literally and figuratively the front door to higher education for students.

Rochester Community and Technical College (RCTC) is Minnesota's oldest community college and one of the nation's oldest original community colleges. It was founded in 1915 when Dr. Charles Mayo made a motion to the Rochester School Board. The Mayo spirit of excellence and innovation is part of the college's culture. RCTC is a national leader in continuous quality improvement and performance excellence through its participation in the Malcolm Baldrige National Quality Award program.

In 1915 the college was located in two rooms in downtown Rochester and served 17 students. Today, on its 518-acre campus, it serves 7,500 students in credit-based enrollments and 3,000 students in noncredit courses. RCTC offers more than 70 credit-based programs and more than 130 credential options in liberal arts, allied health, business, services, and technical career pathways. RCTC ranks among the top four of the 32 Minnesota State Colleges and Universities for online credits taken in the 2006–07 academic year.

RCTC's annual budget is nearly $40 million. The college has experienced tremendous enrollment growth—more than 40 percent—over the past decade. RCTC employs nearly 540 faculty and staff members. Thirty percent of these are full-time faculty members, another 30 percent are part-time faculty members, and 40 percent are staff members and administrators. A 2003 study showed that the college had a regional economic impact of over $80 million.

RCTC works in partnership with other higher education providers to offer students and stakeholders articulation agreements and "2 + 2" career pathways. RCTC also offers programs affiliated with Mayo School of Health Sciences. The college's Business and Workforce Education department provides custom-tailored (contract) training and continuing education serving targeted industries and incumbent workers. In addition, RCTC offers diverse community-based educational programs for youth, including College for Kids, athletic camps and drama and music camps, as well as programming for seniors, including Learning is ForEver (LIFE) and Elderhostel.

Since the early 1990s, nearly $60 million in campus development has occurred, including a new science and technology building, telecommunications enhancements, a regional sports center, and a horticulture technology center. Projects in 2007 include a health sciences building and an athletic field and dome.

Nearly six out of 10 Rochester residents visit the RCTC campus in a single year, and 65 percent have attended or had a family member attend RCTC. Future expansion calls for more community development, workforce partnerships, and the enhancement of kindergarten through grade 14 learning opportunities, making the Rochester Community and Technical College campus a premier educational destination for the region.

Saint Mary's University of Minnesota
Schools of Graduate and Professional Programs– Rochester Center

The Rochester Center of this private liberal arts university's graduate school—one of the largest in Minnesota— holds classes at University Center Rochester's Heintz Center. It serves students through accelerated learning and flexible scheduling, so people who work full-time can earn their bachelor's, master's, or doctoral degree.

Since 1912 Saint Mary's University of Minnesota (SMU) has provided relevant and accessible educational opportunities to those who know their place in the world—and wish to make it a better one.

Established in 1984, SMU's Schools of Graduate and Professional Programs (SGPP) serves 4,300 adult learners in 50 degree and certificate programs.

Saint Mary's adult learners are diverse. Most work full-time and have family and community obligations. They bring a rich variety of life experience to

the classroom, enhancing the SMU learning experience.

A Commitment to Rochester Since 1985

Established in 1985, the Rochester Center now holds classes at the Heintz Center of the University Center Rochester. From a start of 30 students and degree offerings in management and health and human services administration, the Rochester Center enrollment now exceeds 300 students.

Programming is diverse. Adult learners can complete bachelor's degree programs in accounting, business, human resource management, and marketing. They can pursue master's degrees in education, management (including an MBA), counseling and psychological services, health and human services administration, and project management. Advanced graduate certificates are available in educational administration, leading to licensure as a K–12 principal, director of special education, or superintendent. A doctoral program enables learners to achieve an Ed.D. in leadership.

The Mission: Education Outreach
The Vision: Transform Society

As a pioneer in outreach education since 1984, the Saint Mary's SGPP seeks to create communities of learning when and where needed, serving adult learners and addressing the education needs of society.

Serving the educational needs of the Rochester area brought SMU here in 1985 and enabled tenfold growth.

An additional 1,300 students are in the undergraduate programs at the Winona campus's liberal arts undergraduate college. SMU is truly international; nearly 250 students are enrolled at the campus in Nairobi, Kenya, earning degrees in education or African studies.

Saint Mary's vision is simple but bold: To transform society, one learner at a time.

Above left: Bob Funk is Rochester Center Site Coordinator for Graduate Education Programs for Saint Mary's University of Minnesota. Above right: Sue Nelson (left) and Rynn Geier are MBA students at the Rochester Center's Heintz Center. Left: The Rochester Center was established in 1985.

GROWING WITH ROCHESTER SINCE 1985

Saint Mary's University OF MINNESOTA

University of Minnesota Rochester

Students at this university can earn a degree in more than 35 quality academic programs, including new programs that focus on health sciences and biotechnology, which feature research and collaborative educational experiences that integrate professional organizations with the university.

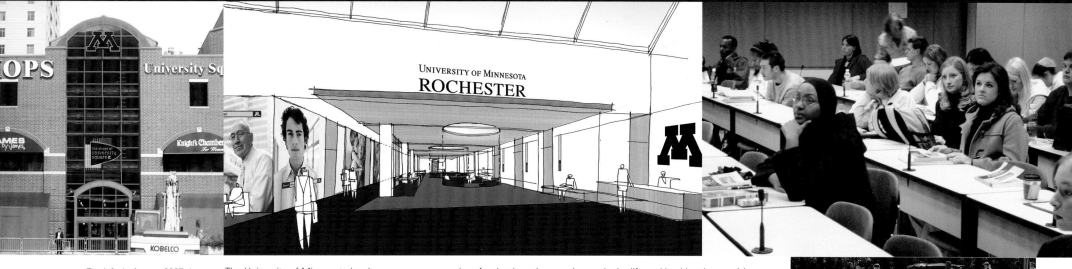

UNIVERSITY OF MINNESOTA
ROCHESTER

Top left: In August 2007 the University Square in downtown Rochester became the new home of the University of Minnesota Rochester (UMR). Top center: UMR is the newest University of Minnesota campus. Top right: Students at UMR learn from world-class professors and can take advantage of high-tech resources. Bottom right: Study groups on campus are also close to Mayo Clinic, IBM, and other leading-edge institutions.

The University of Minnesota has been offering degree programs in Rochester since 1966. In December 2006 the University of Minnesota Rochester (UMR) was designated as the newest coordinate campus of the University of Minnesota system. UMR offers more than 35 high quality academic programs, offering degrees in business, education, graphic design, health sciences, health care administration, public health, social work, and technology. Future programmatic development will focus on bioscience, biotechnology, and the expansion of health sciences

programming. Academic and research initiatives in Rochester promote collaborative relationships with other higher education institutions, as well as with leading health care and technology businesses and industries. These relationships produce unique learning opportunities for students and cutting-edge research opportunities for business, industry, and the university.

Under way at UMR is a center to provide graduate degrees and to generate research in biomedical informatics and quantitative and computational biology

in the life and health sciences. Many educational opportunities at UMR—such as those emerging at this center—will be research-based, innovative, and distinctive.

UMR is located in new facilities in the heart of downtown Rochester. The location promotes collaborations and partnerships with world-class providers of health care and biotechnology companies. The facilities include state-of-the-art classrooms, laboratories, and conference rooms to support the needs of students, faculty, and staff and to

serve the community. Students and professionals study and work in a modern, convenient learning environment.

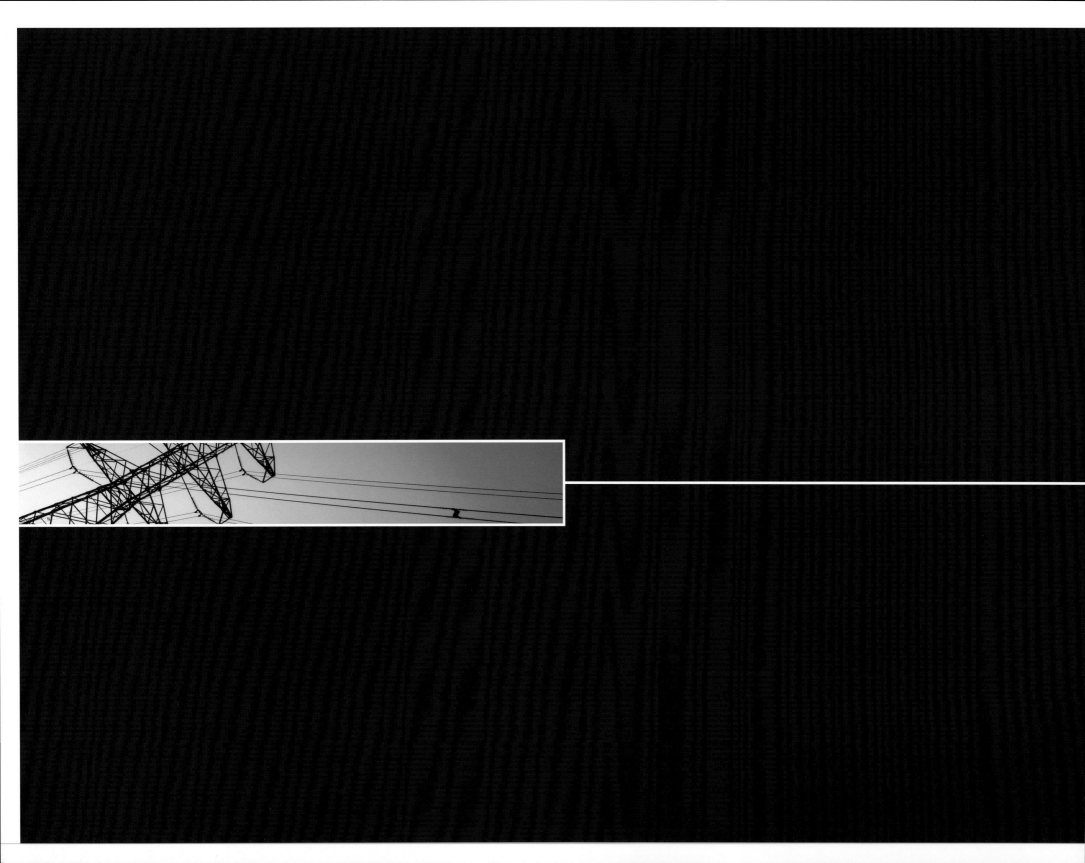

Rochester Public Utilities

This City of Rochester division—the largest municipal utility in the state—has been meeting the community's power and water needs since the 1890s. Keeping ahead of growth, Rochester Public Utilities is increasing its output while minimizing its impact on the environment.

Reliability. That is what customers want from their utility provider, and that is what Rochester Public Utilities (RPU) has delivered for more than 100 years. In 2006 the department pumped an all-time high of 5.07 billion gallons of water and sold nearly 1.3 billion kilowatt-hours of electricity.

With a record 46,433 electricity customers and 35,527 water customers, RPU's operating revenues exceeded $138 million in 2006

($130.7 million for the electric utility; $7.7 million for the water utility). In July of that year, RPU also met a new peak demand for electricity— 288.3 megawatts.

The American Public Power Association (APPA) recognized RPU as a Reliable Public Power Provider excelling in reliability, safety, training, and system improvement. RPU was one of only seven utilities in the country to earn the diamond level recognition, the APPA's highest.

Electrifying History

The utility dates back to the 1890s, with the city's first municipally owned power plant generating electricity in 1894. The water department was created in 1916 with the purchase of a private water company.

William Worrall Mayo, M.D., who founded Mayo Clinic with his sons and the Sisters of St. Francis, had a leadership role in developing the city's electrical and water systems. As mayor of Rochester (1882–1883)

and city councilman, he strongly advocated municipal ownership of public utilities.

After the first electrical plant burned down in 1915, the utility built a plant on North Broadway. A hydroelectric dam and powerhouse on Lake Zumbro that is still in use was put into operation in 1919. And in the 1920s, the young water division, facing shortages, dug four new artesian wells. It also built a 200,000-gallon water tower.

Staying ahead of the city's needs, RPU has grown tremendously. Today, the electric utility's capital assets include a coal-burning steam generation plant, two gas turbines, a hydroelectric power-generation plant, two diesel generators, equipment for providing Mayo Clinic's Prospect Plant with steam, and electric transmission and distribution lines, buildings, and equipment, with a 2006 total value of $138.3 million.

Also at the end of 2006, the water utility had nearly $80 million in capital assets: 18 water storage facilities and 33 wells, plus water mains, pump stations, buildings, and equipment.

Economic Impact

RPU had an economic impact of $259 million on Rochester in 2006 based on the utility's total revenue and its impact on Rochester industries. It employed 193 people, and its operations sustained 400 more jobs, according to Rochester Area Economic Development, Inc. It also provided about $8 million in revenue to the city, saving Rochester taxpayers $8 million in property taxes.

Environmental Impact

RPU always strives to help customers save energy while protecting the environment. For example, an emissions control project under way at the Silver Lake plant is designed to cut emissions of sulfur dioxide, nitrogen oxides, and particulate matter.

Working with customers on energy-saving practices, RPU reduced the city's energy consumption by 10,000 megawatt-hours in 2006. Restaurant owners benefited from a workshop called "Boosting Restaurant Profits with Energy Efficiency," presented by RPU and Minnesota Energy Resources. RPU presents many community courses on energy and technology.

For saving energy and protecting the environment, RPU won the 2007 APPA Award of Continued Excellence for its Demonstration of Energy-Efficient Developments (DEED) program. RPU was a charter member of the DEED program in 1980.

RPU is involved in the multiyear Hybrid Energy System Study, another DEED project, at Quarry Hill Nature Center in Rochester. Working in conjunction with University of Minnesota Rochester, it is developing a revolutionary pollution-free heating and cooling system for both business and residential customers. The system uses two geothermal wells, a hydrogen fuel cell, and a heat pump.

Community Impact

RPU's electric safety presentations reached more than 1,100 students in 2006. Its tree-planting program with the Rochester Park and Recreation Departments planted more than 250 trees—chosen for their ability to grow to maturity without reaching power lines.

Many RPU employees routinely make Meals on Wheels deliveries during their lunch hours. They donate blood and are involved in United Way. They are Scout leaders, service club members, and volunteers in charitable organizations.

Wherever RPU employees are involved, they promise and they deliver.

Above right: RPU employees and their families planted more than 250 trees in 2006. Above center: At the Olmsted County Fair, a line worker demonstrates the power of electricity. Above left: An RPU bucket truck and its crew fix overhead power lines.

Net Cash.

PROFILES OF COMPANIES AND ORGANIZATIONS

Financial and Insurance Services

Merrill Lynch & Co., Inc.

This world-renowned financial institution helped revolutionize the way Americans invest. Today it offers capital markets services, investment banking, advisory services, wealth and investment management, insurance, and banking to its customers in Rochester and throughout the world.

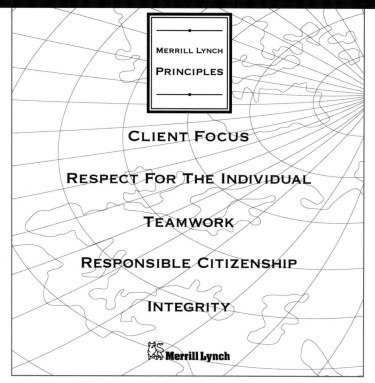

One of the world's leading wealth management, capital markets, and advisory companies, Merrill Lynch & Co., Inc.'s roots date back to 1914, when partners Charles E. Merrill and Edmund C. Lynch combined their talents to form one investment banking firm—Charles E. Merrill & Co. At that time investing was thought to be only for the wealthy, but this innovative firm changed that. One of the company's greatest contributions to the industry was its introduction of stocks and bonds as an investment option for middle-class Americans, democratizing the trade of securities.

Today Merrill Lynch, headquartered in New York City, has offices in 37 countries and territories and total client assets of approximately $1.6 trillion. The company offers a broad range of services to private clients, small businesses, and institutions and corporations, organizing its operations into two related segments—the Global Markets & Investment Banking Group, and Global Wealth Management, which is divided into Global Private Client and Global Investment Management.

As a manager of investments, Merrill Lynch owns about half of BlackRock, one of the largest publicly traded investment management companies in the world, with the job of managing more than $1 trillion in assets. As an investment bank, Merrill Lynch is involved in trading and underwriting securities and derivatives for a wide range of asset categories and is a strategic advisor to corporations, governments, institutions, and individuals.

Merrill Lynch demonstrates its steadfast commitment to clients and shareholders by practicing excellence, integrity, and ethical behavior. It treats client relationships as one of its greatest assets, inspiring the company's board members and 56,000 employees to adopt five guiding principles as the foundation of their actions. These values include a focus on the client, respect for the individual, teamwork, responsible citizenship, and integrity.

At Merrill Lynch, corporate citizenship takes many forms. Among the company's initiatives designed to benefit its communities are global philanthropy transforming lives by giving money, time, and expertise; fostering diversity and inclusion in the workplace; supporting the communities of its clients and employees through sponsorships; reporting on social responsibility and political strategies; bringing financial solutions to underserved communities; and pursuing environmental excellence.

C. O. Brown Agency, Inc.

By following its motto, 'We take time to care,' this agency has provided business and personal coverage for clients in southern Minnesota since 1917, serving all insurance needs. Its agents have the expertise to identify the most suitable policies for individual clients, protecting them from loss at competitive prices.

Clarence Brown established C. O. Brown Agency, Inc. in 1917 with a simple motto: "We take time to care." This set the tone and paved the way to successfully serve clients in southern Minnesota. His son, Robert Brown, continued this philosophy for 40 years. Darwin Olson, current president of C. O. Brown, and the company's 34 agents and 53 staff members continue that solid foundation, treating each client as an individual with unique needs and expectations.

C. O. Brown employees and staff pride themselves on meeting their clients' needs with a number of financially sound, reputable insurance companies. They offer sound direction and advice for all their clients' requirements —both business insurance and personal insurance, including a complete portfolio of health, life, disability, and long-term care insurance.

C. O. Brown's commitment to clients does not stop after they purchase a policy. The agency has its own claims department in-house. If a loss does occur, the C. O. Brown agent stands with the client until the claim is settled.

Olson says, "Our job is to help protect people from loss and then help them put their lives back together if a tragedy or misfortune occurs."

Protecting Businesses

From the outset, C. O. Brown has sold business insurance. Even back in 1917, owning and operating a small business presented considerable risk. C. O. Brown not only understands such risks but also knows how to minimize risk exposure and losses through safety and educational programs. This knowledge has been and always will be the foundation of C. O. Brown's business and reputation. Some of the agency's very first clients are still clients today.

The Right Insurance

Everyone is vulnerable to financial losses from property damage, accidental injury, or acts of nature. The challenge is in determining the right insurance to minimize losses from such events. C. O. Brown is, in effect, a one-stop shop that helps

clients determine the policies that will best protect their business. Agents carefully review the client's insurance needs to prevent duplication or gaps in coverage.

Community Involvement

C. O. Brown employees are involved in their communities. The company encourages participation and

membership in organizations that serve the greater Rochester community and its residents. Olson concludes, "Rochester is a great community with good jobs, good people, and good health care. All of us at C. O. Brown are proud to be part of the Rochester community, and we are proud to help create stability and security for our clients and employees."

Above: C. O. Brown Agency, Inc. owners, from left to right, are: Darwin Olson, Jeff Moat, Lyle Papenfuss, Therese Armstead, and Mike Fogarty.

With a 110-year heritage, it is unsurprising that Ameriprise Financial, Inc. is one of the leading financial planning, asset management, and insurance companies in the nation. This is a company that has built a long record of success on understanding financial priorities and flexibility.

Personalized Financial Solutions for a Lifetime

As an affiliated broker dealer with a nationwide network of more than 10,000 financial advisors, Ameriprise takes a comprehensive, personal approach to financial planning for clients. Considering that just as financial priorities differ from person to person, they also can differ from year to year, Ameriprise helps its clients "shape financial solutions for a lifetime."

Scott DeWitz, a senior financial advisor with Ameriprise, takes the time not only to know his clients personally, but also to know their goals, dreams, and even concerns. Then he takes a unique approach to financial planning called "dream, plan, and track."

DeWitz notes, "I work with my clients to design a personal financial plan around their life goals. I know that everyone's financial picture is different and that priorities change throughout people's lives. I use a unique and collaborative approach to financial planning: define your dream, develop your plan, and then track your progress."

All Ameriprise advisors use similar plans. They help clients define their dreams. Then they tailor a financial plan to suit the client's needs and goals. Finally, they monitor the progress of each plan, ensuring that it stays on track by recommending new strategies as each client's goals change and evolve.

History of Opportunities and Growth

In 1894 John Tappan founded Investors' Syndicate, the company that eventually became Ameriprise. Tappan's vision was of a company that could tailor investment and insurance products for its customers. His dream became a reality as well as a great success story.

By 1937 the company's assets had reached $100 million, and three years later it entered the mutual fund market. In 1984 American Express acquired the company, which had been renamed Investors Diversified Service, Inc. (IDS) in 1949. By 1994, IDS had $100 billion in assets.

Following its own vision to grow, Ameriprise Financial, Inc. separated from American Express in 2005. Just as the company has helped its clients to expand their financial plans for more than 110 years, today Ameriprise is shaping its own future as an independent, publicly traded company. Ameriprise-associated franchisees such as DeWitz develop personal relationships with clients to help them reach their financial goals and feel confident about the future.

James M. Cracchiolo, chairman and chief executive officer, says, "Our primary goal is to be the most sought-after financial planning and services firm. And the best way to achieve that goal is by helping our clients achieve theirs."

Right: Ameriprise Financial, Inc. offers comprehensive and personalized financial planning to help its clients achieve their financial goals.

Ameriprise Financial

thousands

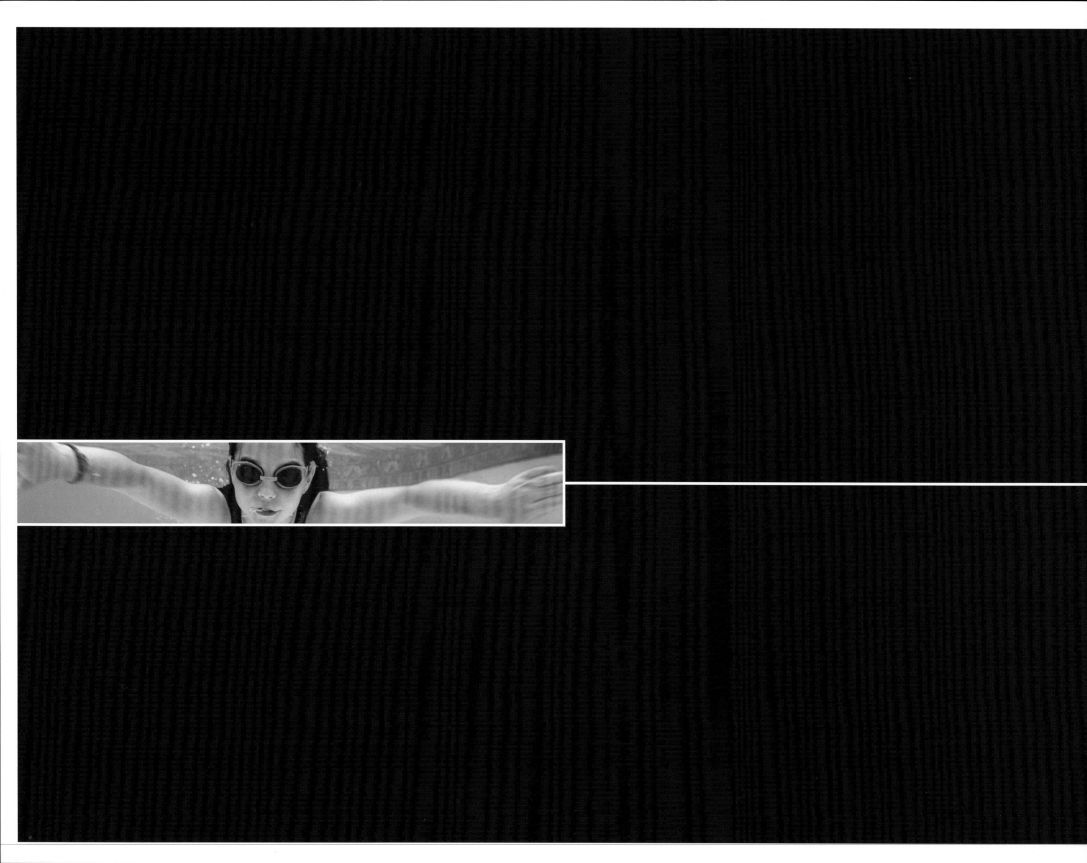

PROFILES OF COMPANIES AND ORGANIZATIONS

Fitness and Athletic Centers

Rochester Athletic Club

Opened in Rochester in 1993, this 260,000-square-foot multipurpose athletic club is one of the largest in the United States. It is a membership-driven business that is committed to quality in its facilities, classes, training, and management and to continually exceeding the expectations of its individual and family members.

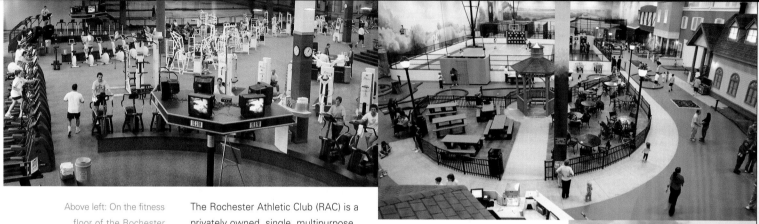

Above left: On the fitness floor of the Rochester Athletic Club (RAC), members can take advantage of more than 125 exercise machines. Above right: In 2006 the RAC opened the Neighborhood—a family entertainment center with 35,000 square feet of sports, games, and other activities dedicated to "families, friends, fun, and fitness." Right: The RAC's outdoor water park features a swimming pool with a water slide. In all, the club has three swimming pools.

The Rochester Athletic Club (RAC) is a privately owned, single, multipurpose fitness facility. The RAC prides itself on the unique offerings its members receive. Members can participate in as many active fitness pursuits as they choose, or they can retreat to the club as a sanctuary, a place to relax and unwind.

Members have access to more than 125 exercise machines available on the fitness floor. The RAC offers over 150 group exercise classes per week, personal trainers, and private and group lessons in many sports and skills.

In 2006 the RAC opened the Neighborhood, which focuses on the family, from toddlers on up. This family entertainment center is designed with village buildings, streets, a café, a park with picnic tables and gazebo, and play areas. The Neighborhood is focused on active play, featuring miniature golf, batting cages, artificial ice for hockey practice, an indoor playground, a gymnasium with Sportwall skill-based games, trampoline basketball, and more, which can be enjoyed by individuals and groups.

The RAC considers the more than 300 associates who operate the club to be one of its major assets. RAC associates have a strong commitment to creating a positive experience for members

and bring a high level of skill and a commitment to service to their work.

The Rochester Athletic Club is truly an in-town sports resort and looks forward to serving Rochester's residents well into the future.

Rochester Athletic Club Facilities

- Fitness floor with over 125 pieces of cardiovascular equipment
- Three full sets of weight machines
- Two spacious free-weight areas
- Swimming pools, including an outdoor water park and, indoors, a 25-meter, five-lane lap pool and a family pool
- Nineteen tennis courts, including 11 indoor courts
- Four high school–size gymnasiums for basketball and volleyball, including two full courts indoors and two full-size sand courts
- Racquetball and squash courts
- Four-lane indoor track, cushioned and banked for running and walking
- Six studios for group exercise, including Pilates and Mind & Body
- The Neighborhood family entertainment center, with miniature golf, batting cages, a playground, a gymnasium with Sportwall, a party area, and more
- Steam room, whirlpool spas, and tanning and massage spa services
- Food and beverage services
- Sport shop
- Meeting rooms

Rochester Swim Club Orcas

Under director and head coach John Sfire, this notable swim club has become one of the most respected in the region, providing unique programs for kids and youth, as well as swimming for fitness and competition for adults—from champions to beginners. Its swim team annually finishes among the top five in Minnesota.

While the Rochester Swim Club has been a fixture in the Rochester community since 1947, it really began making a splash in the 1990s when it added "Orcas" to its name—the Rochester Swim Club Orcas—representing a mascot to which kids can relate. Since then, the club's instructional programs have grown to provide more than 800 lessons annually, and its competitive swimming programs have swelled from 60 to more than 250 competitors.

The driving force behind this tidal wave of growth was and continues to be John Sfire, program director and head coach. Under his leadership, Rochester Swim Club Orcas has become one of the fastest-growing and most respected programs in the area and the upper Midwest. It has the only swim team outside of the metropolitan Twin Cities to compete and finish among the top five teams in the state. In 2003 and 2004 the Orcas 12 and under program was number one in Minnesota and has continued to be among the leaders every season.

Sfire comments, "Rochester Swim Club Orcas provides a healthy activity for swimmers, whether they want to become champions or swim just for fun and exercise. Our goal is to treat every member—champion or beginner—as a winner, while teaching them life skills that will remain with them forever."

The Rochester Swim Club Orcas program provides instruction and training designed to guide swimmers successfully through a curriculum based upon each individual's physical and mental ability and maturity. The club provides an environment where every swimmer can master the proper technique in all four strokes and in starts and turns.

The club's Orcas Masters program accommodates adult swimmers of all levels, from occasional lap swimmers to triathletes and national-level competitors. Its competitive swimming program qualifies athletes for local, regional, and national competitions. Among its notable members are Jim Stewart, known for his National Five-Mile Open Water Championships, and Vince Herring, who has swum around Manhattan Island and was on a relay team that swam the English Channel. Beyond such champions, the Orcas Masters program is truly a place for any swimmer to swim a lot, or just enough.

The club's OrcaKids Swim School is one of the finest learn-to-swim programs in the state. It uses a unique system to teach children ages eight and under all levels of swimming, from water acclimation to skills in advanced strokes. The program's goal includes teaching swimmers to have fun while enjoying the benefits of safe aquatic practices. Taught by accomplished swimmers, along with a professional coach or supervisor, the program focuses on balance, breath control, body position, and stroke technique.

Since it began, the Rochester Swim Club Orcas has had as a foundation its motto, "Traditions of Excellence." Today, the club still follows that motto, offering fun, fitness, and competitive challenges for swimmers of all ages.

Top left and top center: The Rochester Swim Club Orcas competitive swimming program qualifies athletes for local, regional, and national competitions; its teams are among the top swim teams in Minnesota. Top right: Here, John Sfire, program director and head coach, instructs children ages eight and under in the OrcaKids Swim School. The club also offers programs for youths and the Orcas Masters program for adults at every level. Above left: Young swimmers are guided through a curriculum based upon each individual's physical and mental ability and maturity. Above right: Training gives swimmers both technique and safe aquatic practices.

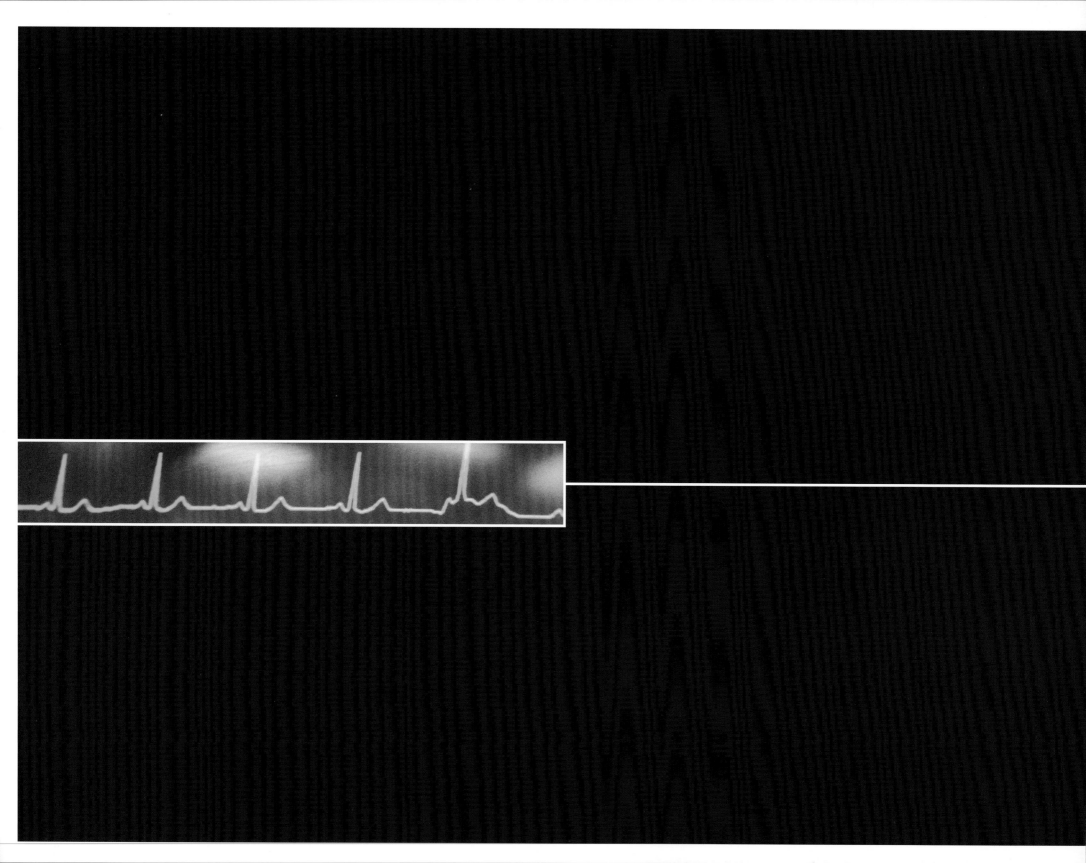

PROFILES OF COMPANIES AND ORGANIZATIONS

Health Care and Medical Technology, Services, and Facilities

Mayo Clinic

A long history of advanced patient-centered clinical care, medical research, and medical education has distinguished Mayo Clinic as one of the world's premier health care institutions. Always at the leading edge of research and practice, Mayo Clinic is advancing such crucial areas as genomics and health care reform.

a specialist at Mayo Clinic with world-class credentials who can help.

Mayo Clinic takes a team-based approach to medicine. For any given patient, Mayo Clinic brings together as many physicians and other health care providers as are needed. These medical experts work hand in hand, consulting with each other, exchanging ideas, and always striving to come up with the best possible solution. Most importantly, they always keep the patient as the center of their focus. This caring approach is not lost on patients, who look for help—and hope—at Mayo Clinic. "They don't stop until they find the answer," said a patient from Sioux City, Iowa.

Above: The atrium of the Gonda Building of Mayo Clinic Rochester is a hub of activity for both patients and staff members.

The needs of the patient come first.

Guided by this simple, essential concept, Mayo Clinic has become the largest integrated, not-for-profit medical practice in the world, and one of the most revered. Over 3,000 physicians and scientists and 46,600 allied staff work at Mayo, which has sites in Rochester, Minnesota; Scottsdale/Phoenix, Arizona; and Jacksonville, Florida. Mayo Clinic also

---

'THE BEST INTEREST OF THE PATIENT IS THE ONLY INTEREST TO BE CONSIDERED.'
— *William James Mayo, M.D.* —

---

serves more than 60 communities in the upper Midwest through the Mayo Health System. Collectively these locations treat more than half a million people each year from the United States and more than 150 countries around the world.

In Rochester, Mayo Clinic and its two hospitals—Saint Marys Hospital and Rochester Methodist Hospital—provide diagnosis and treatment in virtually every area of medicine. No matter how complex the medical problem, there is almost certainly

The high quality care that patients receive is supported by Mayo Clinic's extensive medical research and educational activities. Over 2,500 staff members are engaged in research programs, striving to discover answers that will change the course of diagnosis, treatment, and prevention.

As for education, Mayo Clinic has five distinct schools for physicians, residents, researchers, and allied health professionals. Together, these schools serve more than 3,000 students every year. By operating these schools, Mayo Clinic is helping supply the world with outstanding professionals. In addition, it is spreading the philosophy of a team-based approach to health care that is focused on the needs of the patient.

There are other services, also, such as Mayo Health System, a regional network of clinics and hospitals located in 67 outlying communities throughout southern Minnesota, northern Iowa, and western Wisconsin. Mayo Medical Laboratories, among other services, performs laboratory tests for medical providers worldwide. Mayo Clinic

Medical Transport provides patients with medical transportation by ground, helicopter, or air ambulance. And Mayo Clinic Health Solutions offers a full range of health resources such as newsletters, Web sites, nurse lines, pharmacies, the development of new medical devices, and more.

A Modest Beginning

The history and development of Mayo Clinic is proudly intertwined with that of its hometown of Rochester. In 1863 William Worrall Mayo, M.D., was appointed as an examining surgeon for the Union enrollment board in Minnesota by President Abraham Lincoln. That board just happened to be headquartered in Rochester, so Dr. Mayo moved to Rochester with his family and began practicing medicine.

In 1883 Rochester was hit with a devastating tornado, leaving nearly 40 people dead and more than 200 injured. Dr. Mayo and the Sisters of St. Francis took charge of caring for the injured. This disaster revealed a need for a local medical facility, so the Mayo family joined the Sisters of St. Francis's initiative to build the 27-bed Saint Marys Hospital.

During that time, Dr. Mayo's sons, William James Mayo and Charles Horace Mayo, both received their medical degrees and

eventually took over for their father. As their busy practice grew in the early 1900s, the brothers—known affectionately as Dr. Will and Dr. Charlie—invited other doctors to join them. And the brothers did something else—something unheard of at the time. They also invited researchers, businesspeople, and professionals from a wide variety of disciplines to join the practice. "It has become necessary to develop medicine as a cooperative science . . . for the good of the patient," explained Dr. Will.

Above left: Mayo Clinic offers educational programs and training opportunities to those pursuing careers in medicine, research, and the health sciences. Graduates of these programs go on to practice throughout the world. Above right: Medical research conducted at Mayo Clinic leads to innovations in treating disease and decreasing the burdens of illness.

A Part of the Community

Mayo Clinic and the Rochester community have worked together over the years to help each other grow and evolve. There has been and continues to be a partnership in the truest sense. The city and county work with Mayo Clinic to support the area in a variety of ways—as an employer, as a health care provider, as a significant contributor to the community, and as a provider of charitable care to the underserved.

Financial contributions to community organizations are one of Mayo Clinic's means of support to the Rochester area. Over the years, Mayo Clinic has donated millions of dollars to serve local needs. Within the Rochester area and regional community, these donations benefit a wide variety of programs,

Above, all photos: At Mayo Clinic, physicians and other health care providers work as teams to thoroughly diagnose and treat complex medical problems in virtually every specialty field.

The brothers took their dedication to patients a step further in 1919. Dr. Will and Dr. Charlie, along with their wives Hattie Damon Mayo and Edith Graham Mayo, respectively, donated the assets of the doctors' private practice—and substantial personal savings—to create a not-for-profit medical organization that would be dedicated to excellence in patient care, medical research, and medical education. "The success of

'IF WE EXCEL AT ANYTHING, IT IS OUR CAPACITY FOR TRANSLATING IDEALISM INTO ACTION.'
— *Charles Horace Mayo, M.D.* —

the Clinic," they wrote, "must be measured in its contributions to the general good of humanity." In keeping with this ethic, for nearly 90 years since its establishment, every person who has worked at Mayo Clinic has

been on salary; financial surpluses have been invested in initiatives that advance medical science and education. This ongoing practice is designed to ensure the continued focus on serving the needs of each patient.

including groups working in the areas of accessible health care, diversity, child care, elder care, affordable housing, education, youth programs, public libraries, art, music, and more.

Mayo Clinic's involvement in the community is based, in no small part, on the fact that approximately 30,000 people work for Mayo Clinic in Rochester —and another 39,000 work in jobs at organizations that provide support services to this institution. These people live in Rochester and the surrounding area, raising families and contributing to their communities. By helping to make the community stronger, Mayo Clinic makes Rochester a better place in which to work and live.

Ultimately everyone benefits from this partnership. Mayo Clinic has continually been ranked as one of the top medical institutions in the country by *U.S. News & World Report* and as one of the 100 Best Places to Work by *Fortune* magazine, while the city of Rochester has perennially appeared on *Money* magazine's list of Best Places to Live.

Mayo Clinic's societal contributions extend beyond the city of Rochester and the surrounding area. While it is difficult to quantify in dollars the full extent to which Mayo Clinic fulfills its commitment to society, Mayo Clinic's reach is national and international, and encompasses financially assisted patient care, clinical volunteer work, monetary donations, education, research, and more.

A Bright Future

Mayo Clinic has a history of great success, having helped more than 6.4 million patients since its inception. The past, however, is just that— the past. To remain the vibrant and vital institution that it is, Mayo Clinic constantly looks to—and helps create—the future.

Mayo Clinic relentlessly researches potential cures and medical advancements. It continually educates the new doctors, scientists, and other health care professionals who will help future patients and find tomorrow's cures. It is a major catalyst in pushing for change in the medical industry and in driving advancements in crucial areas such as genomics and health care reform.

In today's world, medicine and health care are changing on an almost daily basis, and Mayo Clinic is constantly changing with them—and often leading the change. One thing, however, will never change at Mayo Clinic: The needs of the patient will always come first.

Above right: A montage symbolizes Mayo Clinic history, which spans the 100-plus years from the days of the horse-drawn ambulance to today's modern medical transport, such as the Gold Cross ambulance. Other conveyances that expedite the arrival of patients who have urgent medical needs include Mayo One helicopter and Mayo MedAir fixed-wing jet airplane ambulances. Above left: Mayo Clinic's Gonda Building is the centerpiece of a multimillion-dollar building project that was financed in large part by philanthropy. Mayo Clinic is a not-for-profit institution with an uncompromising mission to provide the best care to every patient, and philanthropic support enables the fulfillment of this mission.

Precision Chiropractic Center

Since 1995, this unique chiropractic care center has specialized in gentle, non-twisting chiropractic adjusting techniques to relieve pain and improve overall health. With his carefully chosen methods, Dr. Todd M. Sands has helped many people who had given up on ever feeling better.

Above right: Todd M. Sands, D.C., is shown here with members of the experienced and committed staff of Precision Chiropractic Center.

Constant pain in the neck, back, shoulders, and elsewhere can take all joy out of life. If various conventional and alternative therapies have been tried and failed, relief may seem impossible. This is not the case at Precision Chiropractic Center in Rochester, Minnesota, where Todd M. Sands, D.C., has brought relief and healing to many patients with chronic pain. The doctor uses gentle techniques to adjust the spines of his patients. Proper alignment allows for communication between body and brain, and thus healing can take place.

While many chiropractors use forceful twisting methods to adjust patients, Dr. Sands practices a non-twisting approach that allows for better stability. He uses the National Upper Cervical Chiropractic Association (NUCCA) system, along with a chiropractic approach called the Torque Release Technique (TRT). The combination has allowed the doctor to bring relief in some of the most persistent cases.

Dr. Sands, a magna cum laude graduate of the renowned Palmer College of Chiropractic in Davenport, Iowa, has been in practice since 1992 and has owned Precision Chiropractic Center since 1995. He lives in the Rochester community with his wife and three daughters.

Although all chiropractic approaches can provide relief, Dr. Sands specializes in the NUCCA and TRT systems because he feels that they provide the best results. The NUCCA system, which dates to the 1940s, focuses on the first cervical vertebra, the atlas. If this critical area is out of alignment, or in chiropractic terminology, "subluxated," it must be adjusted in a precise manner. Dr. Sands uses gentle pressing on the side of the neck, with the patient lying on his or her side, to realign the atlas. With the complementary system of TRT, Dr. Sands uses an adjusting instrument and light pressure to move the spine back to normal alignment.

Many people—not only those with symptoms—can benefit from upper cervical chiropractic care. In fact, after a lifetime of work, accidents, and sports, most people have some misalignments. Even children may have misalignments. Dr. Sands and his well-trained staff carefully evaluate each patient; the doctor develops an individual treatment plan. Precision Chiropractic Center provides additional information on its Web site (www.precisionchiropracticcenter.net). Many services may be covered by health care insurance.

Subluxations cause many impairments, and Precision Chiropractic Center provides care to help restore health and eliminate pain.

Apollo Dental Center

Founded on a vision of making dental services accessible to patients, this practice has grown to become a thriving business that is one of Rochester's largest and most diverse dental groups and an active player within the community.

Founded in 1996 by the Southern Heights Dental Group of Faribault, Minnesota, this innovative dental practice mirrored medical ideals. Today its owners, Lois Berscheid-Brunn, D.D.S., and Ray Murray, D.D.S., hold to a vision of a dental practice that is accessible to patients because it accepts various insurance programs and offers reasonable fees.

This concept obviously works. Apollo Dental Center has grown steadily to become a thriving business and one of the largest group dental practices in the Rochester community. Today, this practice has five general dentists and one pediatric dentist on staff, as well as an on-site licensed orthodontist. Complementing this team is a professionally trained and licensed staff of registered dental assistants and dental hygienists.

Apollo Dental Center offers a variety of services, including crowns, bridges, full and partial dentures, minor periodontal (gum) treatment, and root canals.

Education and Communication

"Our goal is to educate our patients about their oral health and the overall impact it can have on their general health," states Dr. Berscheid-Brunn. "The education process begins with the patient's first appointment and continues during each subsequent visit."

Dr. Murray adds, "We also believe that communication is key to the education process. Several of our staff members are bilingual in Spanish, and interpreters are readily available through community resources."

Both Drs. Berscheid-Brunn and Murray pointed out that the advantage of a large group practice is particularly evident when it comes to treating entire families. From children as young as age one to geriatric patients, Apollo Dental Center can accommodate the time constraints of busy families by seeing them during a single visit.

Commitment to the Community

Apollo Dental Center's commitment to Rochester extends beyond its patients. This practice has been a major sponsor of the American Cancer Society's annual Relay for Life, the St. John's Center Street Block Party, and various other non-profit organizations. It also supports local high schools and area youth athletic activities.

Additionally, Drs. Murray and Berscheid-Brunn each have strong connections to the community. Both support the dental hygiene and dental assistant programs at Rochester Community and Technical College. They have not only served on advisory committees at the college; they also provide annual scholarships and sponsor internship programs for dental assistant students. Dr. Berscheid-Brunn also serves on the executive board of the Zumbro Valley Dental Society.

Through their dental services as well as their philanthropic work, Dr. Berscheid-Brunn and Dr. Murray, along with their colleagues and staff, care for the well-being of their patients as they do for their community.

Above left: The welcoming offices of Apollo Dental Center accommodate all patients, from children to seniors. The center has five general dentists, a pediatric dentist, an on-site licensed orthodontist, and a caring team of registered dental hygienists on staff.

Samaritan Bethany Inc.

Founded by the Brotherhood of the Evangelical Church of Peace in 1922, this one-time convalescent hotel and hospital, now a family of services, has become one of southeastern Minnesota's leading providers of senior housing options.

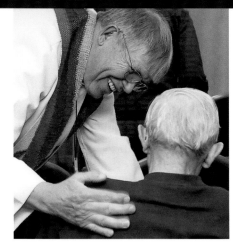

"The Good Samaritan teaches us to reach out to others in need." This is the legacy of Samaritan Bethany Inc. (SBI).

SBI's story begins in 1919, when members of the Brotherhood, a men's group at the Evangelical Church of Peace in Rochester, Minnesota, saw a dire need and pursued the vision. People from all parts of the country needed a place to recover after medical care before returning to their homes. With the blessing of their pastor, Walter W. Bunge, and the enthusiastic support of Drs. William and Charles Mayo, they proposed construction of a "moderately priced" convalescent home for poor people. In 1922, the Samaritan Convalescent Hospital and Hotel, located at 25 Seventh Street NW, was dedicated, turning vision into reality. It included 91 rooms for rent, all of which were outside rooms with one or more windows, and some with private baths.

In 1971, the Brotherhood, later named Christian Fellowship of the Peace United Church of Christ, joined forces with American Lutheran Church congregations to form SBI, combining strengths and experiences, and promoting greater community participation.

The vision continued to expand. Today, SBI offers Samaritan Bethany Heights, a 120-bed, skilled care center set high on a wooded hillside on Assisi Drive. The downtown campus includes Samaritan Bethany Home on Eighth, a 62-bed skilled care center; Samaritan Bethany Terrace Assisted Living on Eighth, with 29 units; and Arbor Terrace, with 66 independent one- or two-bedroom apartments, conveniently attached to the Home on Eighth.

The facilities are governed by SBI in collaboration with seven sponsoring churches: Bethel Lutheran Church, Christ Lutheran Church of Byron, Gloria Dei Lutheran Church, Hosanna Lutheran Church, Our Savior's Lutheran Church, Peace United Church of Christ, and Zumbro Lutheran Church.

Samaritan Bethany Foundation was created in 1982 to heighten community awareness and to raise funds in support of SBI's mission.

SBI's approach for the future includes enhancing the continuum of care for seniors, working towards the greatest possible independence and health for them. The corporation develops programs and services for the residents and continues to move forward for the upcoming generation of elderly. A vision for the future includes a transformation in long-term care and the creation of "household models" for residents.

SBI is one of the leading providers of long-term nursing home care in southeastern Minnesota. It is recognized in the community for its strong emphasis on high quality care and a commitment to excellence.

Benchmark Electronics, Inc./ Pemstar Inc.

This global company provides comprehensive electronics manufacturing services for makers of medical devices and telecommunications, computing, industrial-control, and audio-video equipment. It specializes in leading-edge technologies, expert product design, volume production, and direct order fulfillment.

Pemstar Inc., which was headquartered in Rochester, Minnesota, was founded in 1994 by former employees of IBM. Pemstar quickly grew to provide a comprehensive range of engineering, product design, manufacturing, and fulfillment services to customers on a global basis through a total of 10 facilities strategically located throughout North America, Asia, and Europe. Pemstar excelled in concept-to-customer product development and equipment replication and provided world-class service to companies in the computing, data storage, medical, communications, industrial equipment, defense, and aerospace industries.

Pemstar clients included companies such as Applied Materials, Honeywell, IBM, Fluke, Hitachi, General Dynamics, and Motorola. In addition to its 257,000-square-foot engineering and manufacturing facility in Rochester, Pemstar maintained design laboratories and factories across the world, from Singapore in southeast Asia to San Jose in California's Silicon Valley.

Pemstar achieved annual revenues of $871 million as of March 2006

with about 2,500 full-time workers and 1,600 part-time workers. Among Pemstar's innovative devices is a tiny camera, mounted in a capsule, that is swallowed by a patient and takes color pictures as it works its way through the small intestine.

A Fortuitous Merger

In 2007 Benchmark Electronics, Inc. announced its acquisition of Pemstar. Benchmark is one of the world's foremost electronics manufacturing services (EMS) companies and a major supplier of design services to original equipment manufacturers (OEMs) in the electronics field. Its printed circuit boards and other electronics systems are used in testing equipment, medical devices, and telecommunications and industrial-control equipment.

Benchmark makes its world headquarters in Angleton, Texas, and operates globally, including maintaining significant facilities in Rochester, Minnesota. With sales of $2.9 billion in 2006, it competes effectively against such industry giants as Solectron and Flextronics International.

Benchmark creates integrated solutions in engineering, prototyping and testing, supply-chain management, assembly and manufacturing, testing, final assembly, volume production, and direct order fulfillment for business enterprises. This it does while strategically developing and maintaining close, long-term relationships with customers; focusing on high-end products in growth industries; delivering complete high-volume and low-volume manufacturing solutions around the world; leveraging advanced technological capabilities; and continually identifying cost savings and efficiency

improvements. The company's growth strategy is to continue its global expansion while pursuing strategic acquisitions. Its pricing strategy is to use its worldwide purchasing, design engineering, and manufacturing capabilities to provide its customers with the lowest total cost for the greatest added value.

Benchmark Electronics, Inc. (NYSE: BHE) conducts operations at 24 facilities in nine countries. The company employs nearly 9,000 people and saw its net income grow by more than 38 percent in fiscal 2006.

Left: In 2007 Benchmark Electronics, Inc., which maintains major facilities in Rochester, Minnesota, acquired Rochester-based Pemstar Inc. Shown here is Pemstar's official opening ceremony, in 1994, at which Pemstar founders and Rochester Chamber of Commerce members were joined by Minnesota governor Arne Carlson (front row, second from left). Pemstar founders at the ceremony include (front row, from far left) Al Berning, Bob Murphy, Dan Hughes, and Bill Leary. Pemstar founders not present are Mike Haider, Gary Lingbeck, Karl Shurson, and Dave Sippel.

Prosthetic Laboratories of Rochester, Inc. is dedicated to improving the quality of life for its patients. A privately owned company founded in 1984, the laboratory and its practitioners are dedicated to serving patients who need orthotic and prosthetic care, mastectomy products, and pedorthics. Professional practitioners and skilled technicians combine advanced technology with unparalleled service to restore the greatest possible mobility to their patients.

Prosthetics is the design, fabrication, and fitting of limb replacements, or prostheses, for patients with partial or total limb loss. Orthotics treats patients with disabling limb or spine conditions by designing, fabricating, and fitting devices that support, align, or correct deformities that impair movement. Pedorthics involves customizing or fabricating prescription footwear and related devices, including diabetic footwear and shoes for athletes.

The orthotists and prosthetists at Prosthetic Laboratories work directly with physicians, therapists, and other

professionals to help rehabilitate patients. The laboratory's practitioners formulate recommendations, measure and cast residual and sound limbs, and select materials and components. They are experts in patient fitting, static and dynamic device alignment, gait training, result assessment, and follow-up, all conforming to the physician's directions. They also stay on top of their field through continuing education.

The company's five Silhouette Shoppes in Rochester and Mankato, Minnesota, and La Crosse, Eau Claire, and Stevens Point, Wisconsin, sell mastectomy products. Silhouette Shoppes offer a large selection of breast forms and bras in a boutique setting designed for comfort and privacy. A friendly atmosphere and experienced staff make sure customers receive a proper fitting.

Prosthetic Laboratories of Rochester has nine offices—in Rochester, Mankato, and Brainerd, Minnesota; in La Crosse, Eau Claire, Stevens Point, Marshfield, and Madison, Wisconsin; and in Sioux Falls, South Dakota. The organization, its plant, and its technicians have achieved accreditation and certification through the American Board for Certification in Orthotics and Prosthetics, Inc. (ABC), the oldest and largest organization of its kind.

Southeastern Minnesota Oral and Maxillofacial Surgery Associates

The highly skilled surgeons of this dedicated practice provide corrective and reconstructive procedures for a wide range of dental, facial, and jaw conditions. Serving Rochester since 1984, Southeastern Minnesota Oral and Maxillofacial Surgery Associates combines superior surgical expertise with compassionate patient care.

A long history of surgical excellence and medical service to the community of Rochester distinguishes the Southeastern Minnesota Oral and Maxillofacial Surgery Associates (SEMOMS). Richard Ogle, D.D.S., M.D., founded the practice in 1977 in nearby Owatonna. In 1984 Kevin E. Amundson, D.D.S., M.S.D., moved from the Owatonna office to start a branch practice in Rochester. Since then, this renowned practice has grown to comprise five surgeons and five locations—Austin, Red Wing, and Mankato, Minnesota, in addition to the original two cities. Working with Dr. Amundson are Joel Michelson, D.D.S.; Robert Nustad, D.D.S., M.S.D.; Richard Young, D.D.S.; and Tom Brock, D.D.S. The founder, Dr. Ogle, has retired with the knowledge that his practice is in expert hands.

These skilled and caring surgeons and the professional staff at SEMOMS treat patients with conditions, defects, injuries, and problem aesthetic aspects of the teeth, mouth, face, and jaw.

SEMOMS surgeons come to the aid of patients with jaw misalignments, overbites, underbites, and temporo-mandibular joint disorder (TMJ). These deformities are best corrected working closely with the patient's orthodontist, admitting the patient to the hospital, and then performing surgery. Osteotomies fix the deformity and result in beautiful smiles and facial balance, a life-changing experience for the patient.

For patients who have lost teeth, the surgeons can often fill the gap with implants, which are anchored in the jawbone as permanent replacements. Dental implants have proved superior to crowns, bridges, and dentures. They provide a solid platform for restorations and are done in conjunction with the restorative dental team.

Patients with difficult or impacted teeth that require extraction, with complex medical conditions, or with oral pathology benefit from the skills of SEMOMS surgeons, who routinely treat these situations using the latest surgical and aesthetic techniques.

For many people, fear of pain is a major reason for avoiding oral surgery. That is not a problem here. The doctors at SEMOMS are experts in pain management and skilled in administering anesthetics. Most surgeries are done on an outpatient basis under general anesthesia at the remodeled office at 3632 10th Lane NW in Rochester. Major cases are handled at the Olmsted Medical Center in Rochester.

SEMOMS board-certified surgeons have extensive training. Oral and maxillofacial surgeons complete their training in dentistry and then go on to at least four more years in hospital surgical residency. The SEMOMS group belongs to the American Association of Oral and Maxillofacial Surgeons. And the entire staff is committed to compassionate, personalized care—which includes a unique 24-hour answering service—while also providing state-of-the-art oral and maxillofacial treatment.

Overall, the work of the surgeons and staff at Southeastern Minnesota Oral and Maxillofacial Surgery Associates makes a major positive difference in the health and lives of their patients.

Left: Southeastern Minnesota Oral and Maxillofacial Surgery Associates has five expert surgeons. Standing are (from left) Robert Nustad, D.D.S., M.S.D.; Richard Young, D.D.S.; and Tom Brock, D.D.S. Seated are Joel Michelson, D.D.S. (left), and Kevin E. Amundson, D.D.S., M.S.D.

Pharmaceutical Specialties, Inc.

This Rochester pharmaceutical company develops and manufactures skin and hair care products free of common chemical irritants. For more than 30 years, it has given physicians and their patients effective solutions for special needs, and its products have become widely recommended.

When two Rochester pharmacists set out to develop better products for dermatology patients in 1975, they created a skin care line that would bring relief to millions. For many years, both had worked closely with dermatologists to formulate products for patients with special needs, so they understood the challenges facing physicians and their patients. In the beginning, Pharmaceutical Specialties, Inc. (PSI) was a part-time business venture, but as the demand for its products grew, PSI became a multimillion-dollar business.

PSI develops and manufactures skin care products for people who must or want to avoid common chemical irritants—dyes, fragrance, parabens, lanolin, formaldehyde, and irritating preservatives—that are commonly found in skin care products. Because PSI's products do not contain these ingredients, they are ideal for sensitive skin. Physicians frequently recommend PSI products to patients suffering from dry and irritated skin, psoriasis, atopic dermatitis (eczema), contact dermatitis, and ichthyosis.

PSI products include Vanicream™ skin cream, lite lotion, cleansing bar, sunscreen, and lip protectant; RoBathol™ bath oil; Free & Clear™ shampoo, conditioner, hair sprays, hair gel, and liquid cleanser; and Vitec™ vitamin E lotion. Vanicream, the company's best-known product, is a moisturizing skin cream often prescribed as a compounding ingredient. It is compatible with many drugs and chemicals, has a texture that makes it easy to clean up and package, and is economical for both patients and pharmacists, who may order it in volume. All of PSI's products are available to pharmacies throughout the country from wholesale drug distributors and internationally through PSI distributors in Canada, Asia, and the Middle East.

Over the years PSI has grown steadily as physicians and patients have become aware of its products and their benefits. Leading dermatologists, allergists, pediatricians, major medical institutions, and dermatology training centers use and recommend the company's products for their patients. PSI's founders continue to manage the company and remain involved in developing new products to help people with sensitive skin "break free from the ordinary."

Olmsted Medical Center

A friend of Rochester-region families since 1949, this medical center continues to build its reputation on providing exceptional caring, quality, safety, and service. Its health care unites personal primary care, advanced specialty services, high technology, and a caring touch to deliver outstanding patient care.

Olmsted Medical Center (OMC) began serving Rochester-area residents in 1949 as a small family medicine clinic. Today, more than 140 clinicians provide health care services at 14 patient care locations.

Integrated Health Care

OMC facilities include a multispecialty clinic, a hospital and urgent care center with a 24-hour emergency department, and primary care branch clinics in 10 southeastern Minnesota municipalities. OMC is an integrated community health care provider known for its convenient, expert, and personal primary care, as well as for its more than 20 health care specialties, including plastic surgery, obstetrics and gynecology, and occupational medicine. OMC also is a key partner in research activities for epidemiological studies—studies of factors affecting the health and illness of populations—in Olmsted County.

The Highest Standards

Much of OMC's role as a regional friend of the family blends patient-centered medical technology with a caring touch. An advanced electronic medical records system helps OMC health care providers

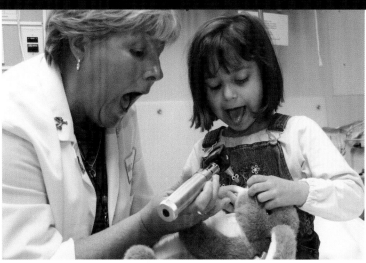

manage more than 250,000 patient visits each year. The system lets clinicians access and securely share patient medical histories, laboratory test results, prescription records, and other information that is essential to providing rapid, accurate diagnosis and treatment. Whether at a family physician's office in one of Rochester's neighboring communities, at OMC's main clinic, or at Olmsted Medical Center Hospital's emergency department or a specialty department, each patient's up-to-date medical history is immediately accessible to OMC's expert health care

professionals. OMC maintains the most advanced medical care innovations, including a growing complement of digitized radiological and diagnostic services.

While OMC has built a reputation on primary care, its facility expansion (from 2004 to 2006) provided state-of-the-art surgery suites, reflecting OMC's commitment to quality specialty care. Each year OMC performs nearly 3,200 major surgical operations. Its surgery suites are designed to handle critical and specialized demands with the most advanced surgical technology while

Olmsted Medical Center Clinical Services

- Allergy and Asthma
- Anesthesiology
- Anticoagulation Clinic
- Audiology
- Birth Center
- Dermatology
- Ear, Nose, and Throat
- Emergency Medicine
- Family Medicine
- General Surgery
- Internal Medicine
- Neurology
- Obstetrics and Gynecology
- Occupational Medicine
- Ophthalmology
- Optical Center
- Orthopedics and Sports Medicine
- Patient Education
- Pediatrics
- Physical Therapy
- Plastic Surgery
- Podiatry
- Psychology and Psychiatry
- Radiology
- Research
- Social Services
- Specialty Surgery
- Urgent Care
- Urology
- Weight Loss and Wellness

ensuring patient comfort. Completely renovated private patient rooms and a new special care unit were part of the expansion. Since 2002 OMC has invested $24 million in capital improvements to benefit patients. OMC provides additional information on its Web site at www.olmstedmedicalcenter.org.

Giving Back

OMC is proud to be an active, caring member of its patients' communities. In 2006 OMC made contributions of nearly $16.5 million to the communities it serves. And many of OMC's nearly 1,200 employees volunteer to assist community-based programs. Through health fairs, preventive health education, public use of OMC facilities, health professional education, research, a migrant health clinic, and other opportunities, OMC continues to demonstrate its commitment to the Rochester region.

Above: Health care at Olmsted Medical Center is personal, blending state-of-the-art medical technology with a caring touch.

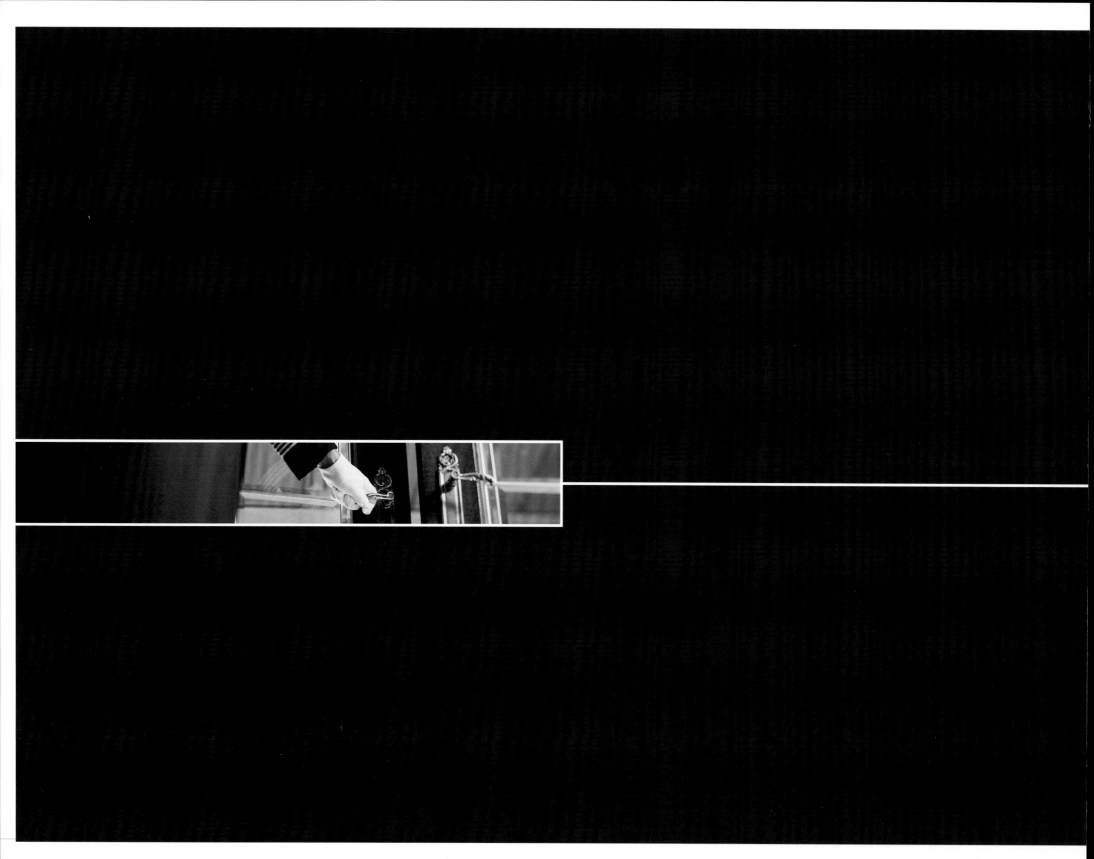

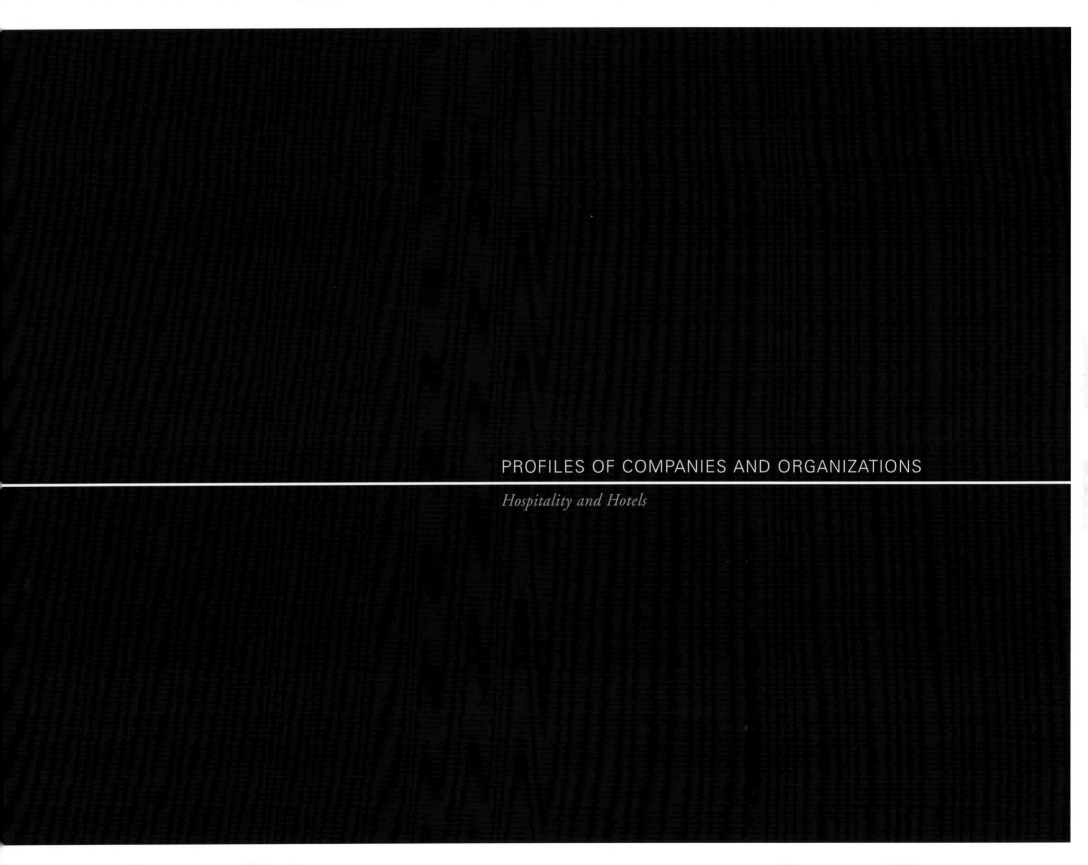

PROFILES OF COMPANIES AND ORGANIZATIONS

Hospitality and Hotels

Kahler Hotels

This company has created the 'healthtel'—a unique synergy of hospitality and health care designed to soothe and delight guests with exceptional accommodations and amenities, a Right Choice menu by chefs and dietitians, and climate-controlled access to dining, shops, and the renowned Mayo Clinic—just what the doctor ordered.

People from all walks of life travel hundreds of miles from home to Rochester, Minnesota, to experience a unique hospitality concept dubbed the "healthtel." It is where world-class patient care goes beyond Mayo Clinic walls to nearby Kahler Hotels to deliver a healthy travel experience.

For decades, Kahler Hotels has consulted with Mayo Clinic to create an array of amenities and accommodations that bridge worldly hospitality with elite medical care. From the 1921 opening of the Kahler Grand Hotel to the 2006 opening of the International Hotel, Mayo Clinic and Kahler Hotels have thrived in a dynamic relationship where both organizations focus on the patient/guest experience.

More than 500,000 outpatients visit Mayo Clinic each year, of whom 80 percent have an average length of stay of more than four days at nearby hotels. Kahler Hotels, with indoor access to Mayo Clinic, accounts for nearly 65 percent of the hotel rooms in downtown Rochester.

Welcoming guests from across the globe, Kahler Hotels provides special rates, upgraded amenities, a Right Choice

Left: The Kahler Grand Hotel was built in 1921 as a hospital with full medical facilities and services along with traditional hotel rooms. Right: Today the hotel provides warm, welcoming public spaces, finely appointed guest rooms and suites, access to restaurant and shops, and climate-controlled passage to the renowned Mayo Clinic.

menu created by Mayo Clinic dietitians and Kahler Hotels chefs, a pharmacy that delivers prescriptions to hotel rooms, 24-hour in-room dining, and a full-service spa and salon. From concierge escort services to and from medical appointments to blood work performed by Mayo Clinic doctors in suites at the International Hotel, Kahler Hotels provides a variety of Mayo-centric amenities.

Kahler Hotels properties—the Kahler Grand Hotel, the International Hotel, Kahler Inn & Suites, the Marriott Rochester at Mayo Clinic, and Residence Inn Rochester Downtown —are all connected directly to the heart of Mayo Clinic via pedestrian subway and skyway. Sunstone Hotel Investors, Inc., a San Clemente, California–based real estate

investment trust, owns and operates Kahler Hotels properties.

The Kahler Grand Hotel is an all-in-one building with underground pedestrian access to all the services a guest needs, including dining options, specialty shops, clothing and accessories boutiques, and more. The 25-room VIP floor at the Kahler Grand Hotel complements

Mayo Clinic's renowned medical services with posh hospitality.

Since opening in 2006, the International Hotel has had an influx of returning guests with overwhelmingly positive reactions to Rochester's first and only five-star service hotel. Guests have included affluent travelers such as rock stars, CEOs, and large entourages from the Middle East. The success led the property to construct six new suites, which were completed in 2007. Room rates for the International Hotel range from $375 to $2,800 a night.

The International Hotel features upscale suites, a telephone call before arrival to determine a guest's needs, personal escort check-in for A-list privacy, satellite television channels and newspapers from around the world, and Ask Mayo Clinic buttons on in-room telephones that provide direct access to Mayo Clinic. Each morning, the hotel rolls out a European-style breakfast with an array of imported foods, such as pastries made in Belgium, European breads, Scottish smoked salmon, hard salamis from Canada, and select French, German, Spanish, and Danish cheeses.

A History of Hospitality

All of this hospitality began in the early 1900s with the vision of two men, William Worrall Mayo, M.D., and John Henry Kahler. Mayo and the congregation of the Sisters of St. Francis, recognizing a need for medical services after a tornado destroyed much of Rochester, opened St. Marys Hospital. Not long after that, Kahler arrived and opened his first hotel, the Cook House, to accommodate the growing needs of patients and guests.

With health tourism on the rise and word spreading that Mayo Clinic was one of the world's elite medical facilities, Kahler built the Kahler Grand Hotel in 1921. An innovative design, the hotel was a 210-bed hospital with operating suites for oral, plastic, and general surgery, as well as a 150-bed convalescent unit and 220 hotel rooms.

Kahler's dedication to top-notch service and hospitality became the foundation upon which Kahler Hotels would operate to this day. At the opening of the Kahler Grand Hotel, Mayo's son William J. Mayo, M.D., stated, "Mr. Kahler has done more for the advancement of Rochester and the Mayo Enterprises than all the rest of the citizens of Rochester put together."

Throughout the 20th century, additional Kahler Hotels properties, such as Kahler Inn & Suites and Residence Inn Rochester Downtown, were built, while the company continued to work with Mayo Clinic to deliver healthy hospitality to guests and patients.

Through a relationship that has been more than 85 years in the making, Kahler Hotels and Mayo Clinic have developed their unique concept that links hospitality and hospitals. To match world-class medical services, Kahler Hotels delivers more than just direct access to Mayo Clinic. It is the little things that distinguish the Kahler Hotels "healthtel."

Above left: The Presidential Suite at the International Hotel features five-star services and exceptional accommodations that continually exceed the expectations of the most discerning travelers. Above right: Pressing the Ask Mayo Clinic button on a guest room telephone at the International Hotel connects guests to registered nurses at Mayo Clinic.

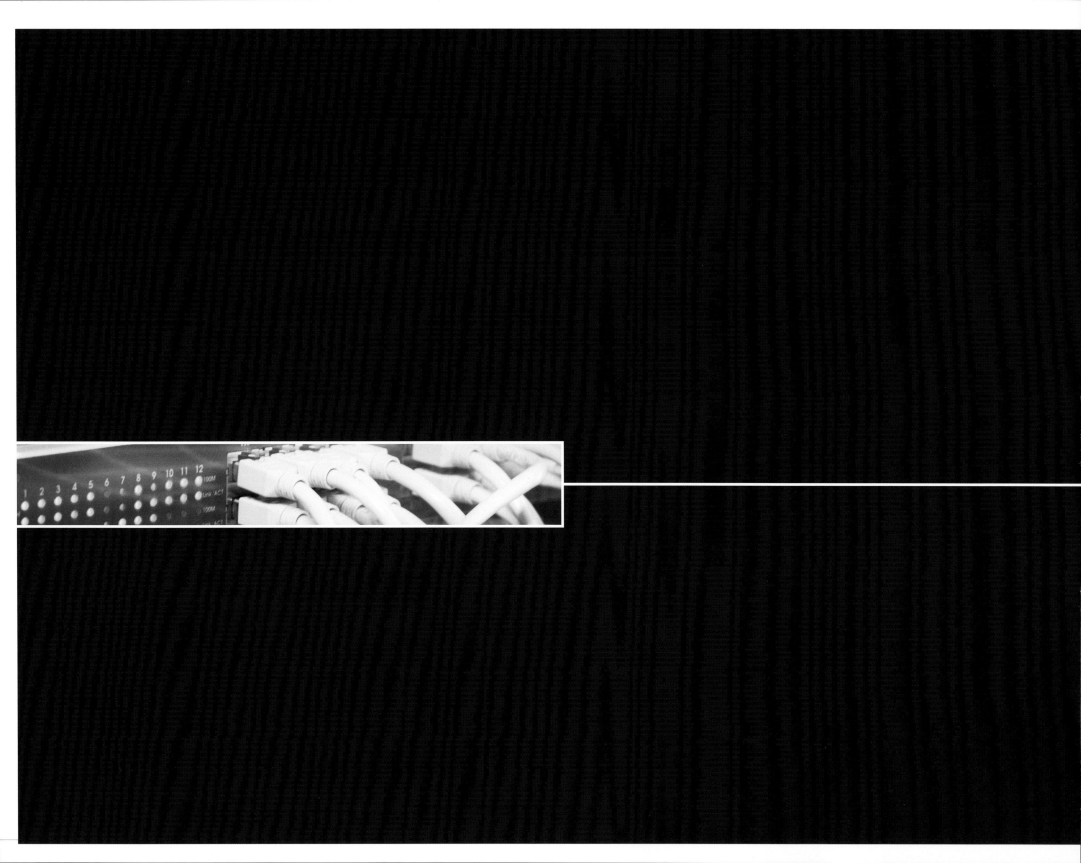

PROFILES OF COMPANIES AND ORGANIZATIONS

Information Technology and Telecommunications

Charter Communications

This premier broadband communications company—the third-largest publicly traded cable operator in the United States—provides a full range of advanced broadband services for the home, including digital television, high-definition television (HDTV), digital video recording (DVR), high-speed Internet access, and telephone.

The year was 1958, and the Abel Cable system was started by the Rochester Video Company, owned by Joseph Porie and A. G. Scheidel. Abel Cable offered customers in Rochester a total of "five channels for five dollars." The cable industry advanced quickly in this technology- and science-driven community—by 1968 Rochester had become one of the fewer than two dozen communities in the nation in which homes were able to receive a full dial of television programming, increasing the number of channels from five to 12.

There have been remarkable advancements in cable—now referred to as advanced broadband technology—since 1958, and today the former

Rochester Video Company is Charter Communications, which offers state-of-the-art cable television as well as high-speed Internet access and advanced telephone services.

Rochester and Charter Communications

Charter Communications (Nasdaq: CHTR) is a leading broadband communications company and the third-largest publicly traded cable operator in the United States. Charter's corporate headquarters is located in St. Louis, Missouri.

Grouped into four divisions nationwide, Charter's organizational structure provides for efficiency and consistency in operations as well as a focus on the importance of operating philosophy and local management.

A unique Charter market area, Rochester serves as the regional headquarters for more than 25 Charter markets and 900 employees located throughout Minnesota and Nebraska. Rochester itself is home to more than 400 Charter employees and to Charter's Minnesota Contact Center. This center serves as a corporate communications resource

for the company, handling inbound customer calls from all over the country and assisting customers with questions they have regarding Charter's products and services, billing questions, and repairs. This Rochester call center responded to more than 1,985,783 calls from customers in 2006.

Portfolio of Services

Charter Communications provides a full range of advanced broadband services for the home, including cable television on an advanced digital video programming platform for digital television, high-definition television (HDTV), and digital video recording (DVR). Also

provided are advanced high-speed Internet access and state-of-the-art telephone services. As part of Charter's continuing focus on enhancing the customer experience, the company was able to begin offering customers the option to bundle all of their communications services and save time and money with the 2006 addition of Charter Telephone.

Moreover, Charter provides business-to-business video, data, and Internet protocol (IP) solutions through its commercial services division, which is known as Charter Business. Advertising sales and production services are sold under the Charter Media brand.

Above right: Charter Communications Rochester employees celebrate the launch of Charter Telephone. Below right: Through the Abel Cable system of Charter Communications' predecessor Rochester Video Company, Rochester became one of the few communities in the United States to have access to a full complement of cable television channels.

February 3, 1967

Abel Cable Expansion Hookups Begin In Northwest Rochester

Ten channel television is available in some northwest Rochester homes today, according to an Abel Cable official. All cable necessary for a system expansion has been strung north of Center Street and that hookups to houses are being made in the northwest sector. Cable line construction will also continue in southeast and southwest Rochester.

Charter
Digital TV • Internet • Telephone

CABLE   INTERNET   TELEPHONE

Philanthropy

One of Charter's largest contributions to the local community is its Cable in the Classroom service, which provides free cable, broadband connections, and access to more than 500 hours of educational programming and online resources to local public and private schools, libraries, and government buildings.

Honored to be a local business, Charter constantly makes charitable contributions and becomes involved with different organizations in the community. Some of the many organizations to which Charter contributes are the Rochester Area Chamber of Commerce, Olmsted County History Center, Rochester Art Center, Hope Lodge, Southeastern Minnesota Initiative Foundation, and local chapters of United Way of America,

the March of Dimes, American Heart Association, Make-A-Wish Foundation of America, and YMCA.

Charter also organizes many special events and promotions to benefit the Rochester community, including

- the annual Holiday Toy Drive Campaign, for which Charter offers a free installation to any new customer who donates a toy during the months of November and December, and all the toys collected are donated to local charities;
- the Hunger Awareness Campaign, for which Charter annually teams up with Channel One Food Bank and Food Shelf in March; during this Minnesota FoodShare month Charter helps to raise awareness about hunger in southeastern

Minnesota and to collect food at the local office by offering customers a free pay-per-view, on-demand movie; and

- serving as a sponsor for local minor league teams, including Rochester Honkers baseball and Minnesota Ice Hawks hockey; as a professional sports sponsor, Charter helps to coordinate local visits by the Minnesota Twins and the Minnesota Wild by providing funding, advertising, and special events for the teams.

Charting the Future

Since 2000 Charter has invested millions of dollars to build and upgrade local cable infrastructure. Charter's infrastructure consists of a state-of-the-art combination of fiber-optic lines and coaxial cable. Charter plans to continually invest in upgrading its infrastructure

in order to deliver the most up-to-date products and services.

As digital technology melds video, audio, and voice communications with personal computing and the Internet, Charter's goal is to make the "wired world" accessible to as many people as possible. Charter continues to realize new efficiencies from a more uniform approach to service deployment, pricing, customer procedures, and technical operations. Charter is also implementing modern call centers that feature sophisticated tools and technologies in support of employee training, call monitoring, and service analysis.

In these and other ways, Charter Communications is helping to chart the future of its industry.

Above left: Charter Communications employees pack up hundreds of toys to be donated to local charities as part of Charter's annual holiday toy drive. Above right: Charter raises thousands of dollars at the annual Women Rock! Girls & Guitars concert, which raises funds for the National Breast Cancer Coalition Fund.

IBM Rochester

This company's leading development and manufacturing center in Rochester is responsible for advancements in engineering design, gaming technology, life sciences technology, and supercomputing development. It is aligned around the single, focused IBM business model: innovation.

Above and right: IBM began operations in Rochester in 1956 in a 50,000-square-foot facility with just 174 employees. Today it has expanded to 3.5 million square feet—the largest IBM facility in the world under one contiguous roof—and more than 4,400 employees. IBM is Rochester's second-largest employer (after Mayo Clinic) and Minnesota's largest information technology (IT) employer. Right: The IBM System i is an all-in-one IT platform offering powerful, efficient computing solutions for businesses of all sizes.

IBM in Rochester, Minnesota, has a rich heritage of business computing innovation and client satisfaction—a tradition that began more than 50 years ago, in 1956. With a focus on the development of systems and services, IBM Rochester employees work together to provide innovative computing solutions to clients around the world.

Development, Manufacture, and Support

While IBM Rochester offers a wide diversity of employee skills, its predominant mission is the development, manufacture, and support of IBM's collaborative business systems. IBM Rochester employees play a vital role in the development, manufacture, and client support of the IBM System i, the company's popular business computing system for large enterprises as well as small to midsize businesses. The ability of IBM Rochester's manufacturing organization to innovate and deliver has enabled it to add to its line the manufacture of the IBM System p—a powerful and technologically advanced line of UNIX servers—as well as self-checkout systems for the retail sector.

The IBM Customer Solution Center (CSC) in Rochester provides a single source to develop, prototype, manufacture, configure, and ship custom-designed solutions for clients worldwide. The CSC provides clients services such as assembling hardware, loading software, performing functional tests, and packaging and shipping clients' products.

While the development and manufacturing of business systems plays a significant role at IBM Rochester, the development of new software remains fundamentally important. IBM Rochester employees are a part of IBM's market leadership in developing information management software, application integration tools and middleware, and systems operations and systems management software.

Engineering Solutions for Clients

Over the years IBM Rochester has expanded to become a leading development facility. It is responsible for advancements in engineering design, gaming technology, life sciences technology, and supercomputing development.

In 2002 IBM formed a business that offers IBM know-how and capabilities in information technology (IT) services and advanced technology directly to its clients. Global Engineering Solutions offers clients a wealth of engineering talent who can leverage IBM's advanced technologies and vast intellectual property—including designs ranging from complex microchips to entire computing systems—to meet clients' customized business and product needs.

The work of IBM Rochester engineers has resulted in innovative new products such as a handheld device for traders on the floor of the New York Stock Exchange, a hands-free wearable computer, and collaboratively developed medical devices and programs for leading health care and life sciences institutions.

State-of-the-Art Innovation

IBM is aligned around a single, focused business model: innovation. While IBM remains committed, as ever, to lead the development of state-of-the-art technologies and the products and service offerings built around them, the company measures itself today by how well it helps clients solve their biggest and most pressing problems.

IBM Rochester engineers work closely with their colleagues at IBM Research on the development of supercomputers such as Blue Gene/L. Each Blue Gene/L rack is manufactured and tested in Rochester and then shipped to government,

business, and research clients around the world. Blue Gene/L has claimed the number one spot numerous times as the world's fastest in the highly respected Top500 ranking of the world's most powerful supercomputers. IBM Rochester also is home to a Blue Gene Capacity on Demand Center, which allows businesses and research institutions flexibility and choice in acquiring computing time on a supercomputer.

IBM also has achieved the triple crown of the gaming world, with IBM-developed computer processor architecture being the choice of today's top three gaming platforms—Microsoft, Nintendo, and Sony. IBM Rochester engineers and their colleagues and business partners around the globe designed, developed, and delivered custom-designed microprocessors that are found in millions of video game consoles produced by these companies.

Corroborating success stories like these is the record-breaking number

of patents earned in a single year by IBM—3,631 U.S. patents in 2006—extending IBM's record to 14 years as the world's most innovative company based on patents earned. Over the years, IBM Rochester inventors have contributed more than 3,000 patents to the IBM portfolio. IBM translates these technology advances into value for its clients around the world.

Community

Innovation and commitment also exist at IBM beyond the realms of technology, in its employees' generous support of the communities in which they live. In

2006 IBM Rochester employees contributed more than $1.6 million through the IBM employee charitable contribution campaign. Beyond dollars, employee volunteerism is a corporate tradition. IBM's dedication to kindergarten through 12th grade and higher education has benefited thousands of students through gifts of technology, volunteerism within the classroom, and employee participation in IBM e-mentoring programs and technology camps for students. Each year, IBM Rochester employees contribute an average of 113,000 volunteer hours to schools and nonprofit organizations in the region.

Top left: IBM's Blue Gene/L supercomputer—named the world's fastest—handles vast amounts of data in seconds. IBM and its partners are exploring many high-performance applications for Blue Gene/L, including life sciences, financial modeling, hydrodynamics, quantum chemistry, molecular dynamics, climate modeling, and astronomy and space research.

Top right: The Cell processor, "a supercomputer on a chip" jointly developed by IBM, Sony, and Toshiba, has a multicore design with high-speed communications capabilities and delivers up to 10 times the performance of a personal computer chip.

Above right: In 1956 the IBM Rochester workforce shows the IBM 077 Numeric Collator, which processed a then-revolutionary 240 punched cards per minute and was the plant's first manufacturing responsibility.

Ideacom Mid-America

Providing unified communications systems, this company offers clients a long tradition of excellent service combined with advanced products—including wired and wireless Voice over Internet Protocol (VoIP)—that are built to enhance operations and profitability.

Above: Ideacom Mid-America is a major converged communications systems provider, specializing in health care communications, Internet Protocol (IP) telephony, wired and wireless data infrastructure deployment, and data security and storage.

Ideacom Mid-America is a major communications systems provider, a position that has been well earned. The company is a product of more than 50 years of successful implementation of communications systems that deploy converged, wired, or wireless solutions, including Voice over Internet Protocol (VoIP).

Ideacom originated in 1954 as Executone Systems of St. Paul.

Beginning in the early 1990s, the company expanded its operations geographically, and today it serves the upper Midwest. Its territory is supported by offices in Rochester, St. Paul, Minneapolis, Des Moines, and Milwaukee. Ideacom attributes its growth to its focus on customer service, which is provided by a large staff of certified technicians and customer-training staff members.

In January 2001 the company changed its name to more accurately reflect its expansion in territory and in product offerings from world-class manufacturers. Ideacom offers clients the best of two worlds—a long tradition of excellence in service and support combined with new ideas and technologically advanced choices in communications systems and software.

"Our company began serving the health care and commercial facilities in the Rochester area in the early 1960s," says Larry Anderson, president of Ideacom Mid-America. "By 1990 it was clear that we needed a full-time Rochester office to support our sales and service staff and our large base of health care, government, and business clients. The Rochester office was opened in 1991."

Providing Clients with the Power of Partnership

Ideacom products and services are provided through two key divisions—Converged Technology and Health Care.

The Converged Technology division applies a total-solution management approach in working with clients to supply the telecommunication systems they need. The Ideacom staff completes a needs analysis of its client's requirements for local and long-distance telephone and Internet services, as well as the client's communications systems hardware and software needs. Ideacom then builds the most efficient and effective communications systems for the client's enterprise, providing a full range of networked communications solutions that offer voice, data, and video systems and the network services to support them.

Ideacom's Health Care division works in partnership with Communications Mid-America (CMA), providing communications solutions that are specialized for its health care–provider clients, including most major medical facilities in Minnesota and Iowa. Ideacom and CMA offer complete systems support, from consultation services to installation to ongoing technical support for clients at all types of health care facilities, including acute care, long-term care, and assisted living. CMA provides complete turnkey communications and security solutions, consisting of wired and wireless telephone systems; specialized call systems for nurses; and patient-monitoring, intercom, and paging systems.

The Ideacom family of companies also includes PCS Technologies, a leading integrator of wireless data systems that builds wireless broadband-access systems, including tower development and installation nationwide.

Ideacom Mid-America continually evolves, supplying its clients with reliable, next-generation communications systems. It will keep growing and changing along with the newest technologies in order to provide clients with the best communications systems available.

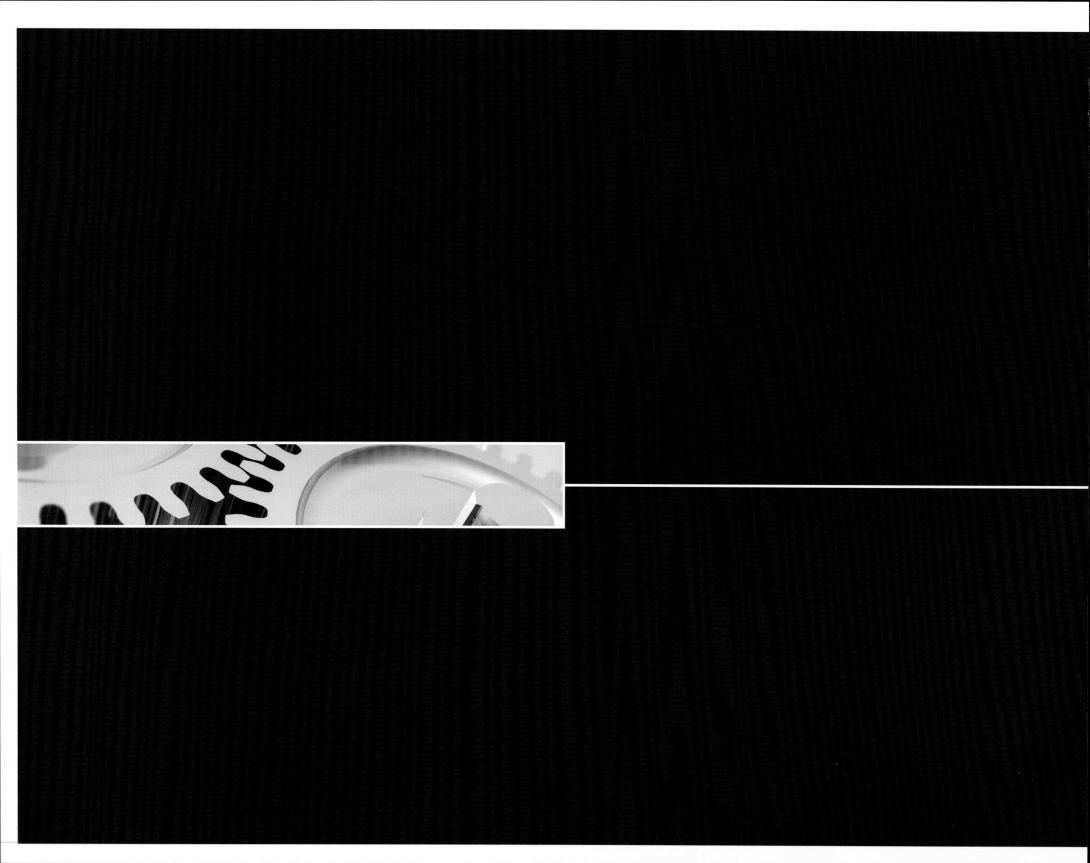

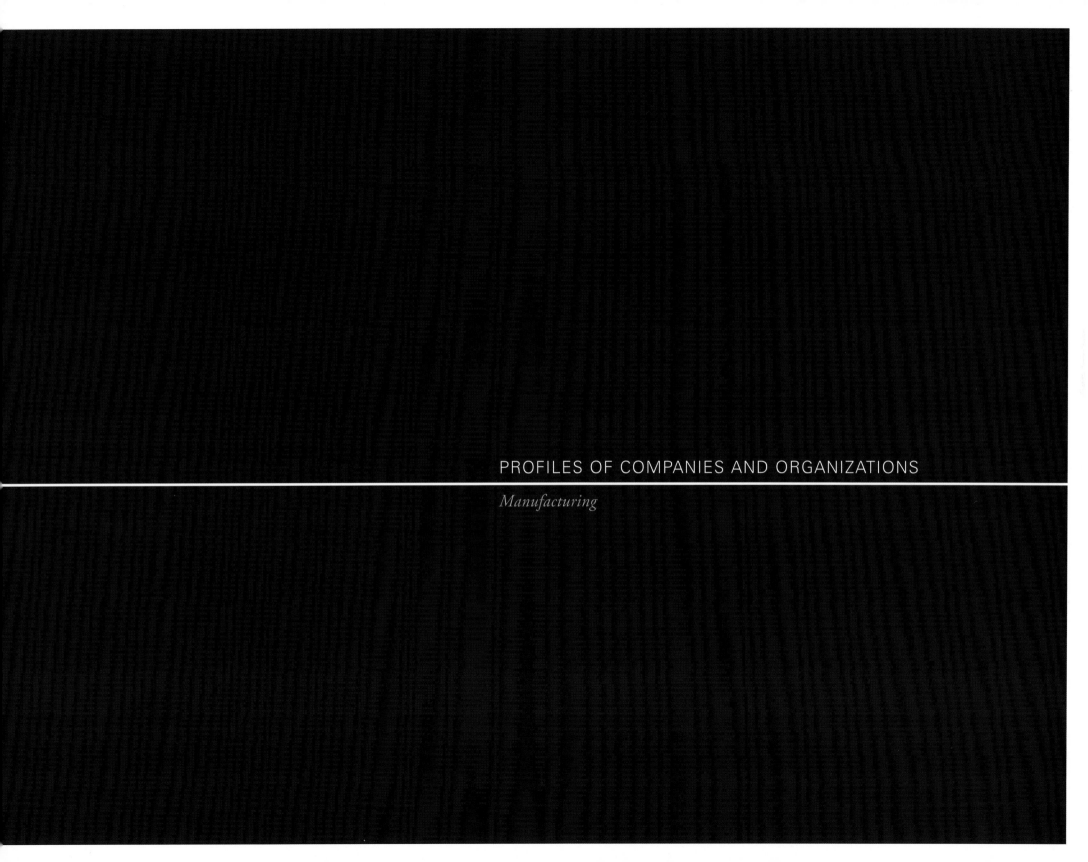

PROFILES OF COMPANIES AND ORGANIZATIONS

Manufacturing

McNeilus Corporation

This leading manufacturer of concrete mixers and refuse truck bodies creates products designed for the toughest environments. The company is noted for its high quality products and service, its environmentally responsible ethic, and its continual creation of industry-first innovations in productivity and safety.

McNeilus Corporation, headquartered in Dodge Center, Minnesota, is a world-class manufacturer of mobile ready-mix concrete mixer trucks and refuse truck bodies. McNeilus® Standard and Bridgemaster® concrete mixers have long set the bar for job-site performance and reliability, while the McNeilus® line of refuse trucks is found in major refuse-hauling fleets throughout the United States and Canada. The McNeilus rear-loader refuse truck is highly regarded among customers and competitors alike for its quality, its rock-solid reliability, and its toughness. And McNeilus is a leader in both industries by driving change through innovation—such as its Revolution® composite mixer drum and its AutoReach Automated Side Loader® with articulated arm.

Right: McNeilus Corporation's McNeilus Revolution® composite mixer drum allows a 2,000-pound-greater legal payload compared to a standard steel mixer drum. The product also decreases vehicle weight and reduces noise.

'The Customer Is Our Boss'
McNeilus started building concrete mixers because there was a need that was not being met by other manufacturers in the industry. Garwin McNeilus, the founder of the company, instilled a philosophy of listening to customers, specifically listening for the wants and needs of ready-mix concrete producers who needed to do more than their equipment allowed. McNeilus incorporated the company in 1970. And beginning on the very first day, every McNeilus team member answered to the same boss: the customer. This approach toward product development and customer service quickly put McNeilus on the map.

It also was one of the reasons that Oshkosh Truck Corporation acquired McNeilus's company in 1998. Oshkosh Truck's philosophy, too, is to understand the rigors of customers' jobs and to deliver vehicles and vehicle bodies designed to outperform anything else on the market.

And because the companies' motivations were in line with each other, the acquisition of McNeilus's company by Oshkosh Truck was a natural fit.

McNeilus products are designed to thrive day in and day out in the toughest environments, matching the demands

of the customers who depend on McNeilus concrete mixers and refuse truck bodies for their success. That commitment to quality and innovation is mirrored by the service and support system created to keep McNeilus fleets on the road. And such commitment is the reason McNeilus is North America's largest manufacturer of concrete mixers and refuse products.

A Matter of Pride

There is a pride at McNeilus that visitors can easily sense when they walk alongside the assembly line. The craftsmen and craftswomen that make McNeilus products are passionate about what they do. In fact, in many areas of the facility employees sign their names on the drum or fixture before it passes on to the next station. This is integral to McNeilus's quality process, as it is proof that each employee feels that he or she plays a valued role in the engineering, design, and manufacturing of every product and the subsequent success that product has for the customer. Each of McNeilus's 1,800 employees nationwide, from assemblers to welders, engineers, painters, and designers, embraces his or her role in making a difference in the productivity and safety of the customer. To assure quick response and attention to customer needs, McNeilus has 20 branch locations, 57 authorized service centers, mobile service, round-the-clock response, and a toll-free hotline.

A Tradition of Innovation

The Revolution composite mixer drum, launched in 2003, changed the ready-mix industry by increasing payload, reducing vehicle weight, and reducing noise. The Revolution drum is perhaps the greatest advancement in the ready-mix industry since mixers were first mounted on trucks. This state-of-the-art composite mixer drum is 2,000 pounds lighter than a steel drum of similar size, thereby allowing a 2,000-pound-greater legal payload.

Above left: This standard mixer, introduced in 1976, was among the first to be completely manufactured by McNeilus. Above right: A larger, "East Coast" model standard mixer is used in New York City.

153

Above left: McNeilus front-loader refuse trucks at the Hubert H. Humphrey Terminal at Minneapolis–St. Paul International Airport are being loaded into a Russian AN-24 aircraft headed for Bosnia in 1996. Above right: The McNeilus Tag-Axle rear-loader refuse truck allows for maximum payload and weight distribution—ideal for use in states with more-stringent weight laws.

This equates to an additional one-half cubic yard of concrete for every pour. Also, lower vehicle weight when returning from a job site contributes to increased fuel economy and reduced environmental impact.

Shared Technologies

The Revolution composite mixer drum is also available for the Oshkosh S-Series™ front-discharge mixer truck and is just one of the shared technologies that keep McNeilus and Oshkosh Truck in the forefront of their respective industries. Nonmetallic water tanks, hydraulic tanks, and control systems are but a few of the innovations McNeilus and Oshkosh Truck have developed to help make customers' jobs easier, safer, and more efficient. A prime example is the nonmetallic water tank introduced by McNeilus in 2007. Customers have an option to shave more than 200 pounds from a load, compared to the weight of a similar steel tank. Similarly, the nonmetallic hydraulic tank, which is an optional feature, is 60 pounds lighter than the standard steel hydraulic tank and provides better flow and filtering.

Such innovation is not limited to drums and water tanks. The McNeilus AutoReach Automated Side Loader truck features a patented AutoReach® arm, the first such articulated arm in the industry. McNeilus's Street Smart Parts™ is an innovative approach to supplying replacement parts, offering customers the opportunity to order replacement parts online directly from the manufacturer. The site includes three-dimensional drawings of parts and provides a downloadable catalog.

A great deal of quality design and engineering is invested in striving to ensure that McNeilus truck bodies offer exceptional durability and longevity. In fact, McNeilus was one of the first companies in its industry with a manufacturing system certified to International Organization for Standardization (ISO) 9001:2000 standards for all of its products. And to back up its products, McNeilus fields one of the largest, most extensive service and support networks of branch offices and authorized service centers in the industry.

Focused on Safety

McNeilus has always viewed its industry with an eye toward innovation. Its innovations sometimes take the form of products and initiatives designed to make the industry safer.

In 2007 McNeilus and Oshkosh Truck led the ready-mix industry in vehicle driver safety by offering a new side air bag and active safety restraint seat belt system for concrete mixer

community service organizations, are partners in change, and help a broad range of people and organizations.

Outstanding Lineage

Oshkosh Truck Corporation acquired McNeilus in 1998 not only because of its leading market position, which it continues to hold today, but also because it is a specialty manufacturer of specialty vehicle bodies. Oshkosh Truck views McNeilus as an ideal strategic fit—one that leverages corporate synergies and expertise in severe-duty application design to drive industry-leading innovation and product development.

Oshkosh Truck is a leading manufacturer and marketer of specialty vehicles and vehicle bodies for five primary sectors: defense, concrete placement, refuse hauling, specialty access, and fire and emergency. It is a company that is broadly diversified, and it makes use of proprietary technologies to create powerful competitive advantages across a variety of markets.

In fiscal 2006, Oshkosh Truck achieved $3.43 billion in sales and delivered a 10th consecutive year of improved financial results. With the acquisition of JLG Industries by Oshkosh Truck in 2006, revenue is expected to reach or exceed $6 billion annually.

trucks. The Side Roll Protection System, designed in conjunction with the LifeGuard Technologies division of IMMI (Indiana Mills and Manufacturing, Inc.), introduced an advanced level of driver protection, the first-ever of its kind. This system automatically senses a truck beginning to roll over and deploys a seat-mounted air bag to protect the driver, while an automatic seat belt tensioner pulls the driver down into the seat, providing increased distance between the driver's head and the side of the truck cab. The system is available in the Oshkosh Truck S-Series

front-discharge mixer truck and also will be offered in McNeilus mixer trucks.

In 2005 McNeilus teamed up with a large private refuse hauler and the National Solid Waste Association of North America to begin a public awareness campaign aimed at protecting refuse haulers who work on busy streets. The "Slow Down to Get Around" campaign, which involved the development of public service announcements for television and radio, brochures, vehicle graphics, and various speaking engagements,

educated the general public about slowing down when approaching refuse trucks on their routes. Several large cities and national fleets quickly recognized the potential danger and the opportunity for positive change and adopted the campaign's message.

Sense of Community

McNeilus is deeply rooted in serving the community and demonstrates this commitment by being a strong supporter of United Way. By giving to United Way, McNeilus and its employees touch a myriad of

Above: The Oshkosh Truck Corporation's S-Series™ front-discharge concrete mixer truck is the leading brand of front-discharge concrete mixer trucks in the industry.

Gauthier Industries Inc.

Building on more than 60 years of experience in the metal fabrication industry, this innovative Rochester company incorporates the most advanced equipment, the highest standards of quality assurance, and a skilled workforce to exceed its customers' expectations.

Above: Gauthier Industries Inc. has the expertise and versatility to produce a wide range of metal fabrications, stampings, contoured and angular components, electronic cabinetry, electrical enclosures, and much more.
Right: Gauthier, which is proud to be headquartered in Rochester, contributes to the local and regional economy as a major employer and an industry leader.

Gauthier Industries Inc. is a versatile, full-service, world-class metal parts manufacturer that has achieved a leading position in the marketplace through the vision of its leaders and the hard work of its employees.

Gauthier's core processes are supported by the most advanced equipment, engineering, powder coating, and assembly; an ISO 9001:2000–certified quality-assurance program; and a modern, 100,000-square-foot facility. Founded in the 1940s by Emil Gauthier and partners, the company is an accomplished metal parts provider with six decades of experience that can be seen in all of its processes, from the design stage to delivery of the completed product.

Gauthier can fabricate contoured and angular components on time, at low cost, and with high quality results. For contoured parts, a variety of techniques are used, including radius forming. The company also uses high-speed, precision laser cutting; computer numerical control (CNC) fabricators; press brakes with CNC back gauging; and tungsten inert gas (TIG), metal inert gas (MIG), and spot welding.

Gauthier also has the versatility to produce a wide variety of stampings and perform other machining operations, such as double-disc grinding and honing. The company makes a variety of precision sheet-metal parts, including electronic cabinetry and electrical enclosures built to the customer's precise specifications.

Gauthier fabricates small and large parts accurately and efficiently. Advanced sheet metal capabilities are achieved with laser cutting, CNC turret presses, and a state-of-the-art programming software system. The laser cutting systems have full-sheet capacity, which eliminates the need for a shear operation, reduces setup time, and requires no special tooling—making it ideal for prototyping and fast turnarounds. The CNC turret presses with auto index stations enable the company to make odd-shaped contoured parts, some of which may be inexpensively modified to meet changing design requirements.

Gauthier's quality-assurance procedures are designed to make sure that Gauthier products meet or exceed specifications and to ensure on-time delivery. Large production runs are accommodated by skilled production workers, and constant awareness of customers' production schedules leads to prompt deliveries and lower costs.

Dave Kocer, owner and CEO of Gauthier Industries, notes that "innovation, adaptability, and a strong work ethic have been the keys to Gauthier's longevity." The company successfully works with clients to achieve the best components possible at the lowest cost. In this way, customers gain a competitive edge in the marketplace, and Gauthier Industries continues its tradition of outstanding service and superior products.

Foldcraft Co.

From the world's largest foodservice chains to the most upscale restaurants, all kinds of dining establishments are furnished by this Minnesota-grown manufacturer of booths, tables, chairs, millwork, and décor. Fully owned by its employees, the company operates three factories—two in Minnesota and one in California.

What began as Harold Nielsen's one-man woodworking shop in 1947 is now one of the nation's largest manufacturers of foodservice furnishings and décor. Foldcraft Co., based in Kenyon, Minnesota, produces a full array of furniture for restaurants and cafeterias. With customers that range from some of the largest quick-service restaurant chains in the world to some of the finest dining establishments in the country, Foldcraft has established a diversified base of business through the years.

Today, Foldcraft operates out of three manufacturing locations. Kenyon, home of the company's corporate headquarters, serves as the hub and as the manufacturing site for Foldcraft's Plymold brand of seating and décor products. Complementing this operation is a custom millwork operation in Corona, California, and a millwork and upholstery operation in Bloomington, Minnesota.

Foldcraft conducts business under three major divisions. Plymold, the oldest of these, was established in Kenyon in 1969. The primary

product lines of Plymold are upholstered seating, contour laminate seating, wood booths, cluster seating, tables, chairs, cabinets, and related décor. Foldcraft's California operation, WB Powell, Inc., produces some of the finest quality commercial millwork on the West Coast. WB Powell installations can be found in hotels, churches, spas, and restaurants.

Foldcraft's Bloomington operation manufactures cabinetry, upholstered seating, and architectural millwork for foodservice industry interiors. Collectively, the operations of Foldcraft can produce the complete package of furnishings and décor required by any foodservice establishment. Foldcraft's products can be found installed around the world.

A proud member of the southern Minnesota business community, Foldcraft has the added distinction of being completely employee-owned. Thanks to an ESOP (employee stock ownership plan) that has been in place since 1985, Foldcraft's employees have the privilege and responsibility of owning and growing their company.

Left: Foldcraft Co., a wholly employee-owned business, is guided by (standing, from left) Bill Proesch, vice president of sales and marketing; Donald Archibeque, vice president of design-build operations; Douglas Westra, CFO; Charles Mayhew, president, CEO, and chairman of the board; and (seated) Brian Kopas, vice president of operations.

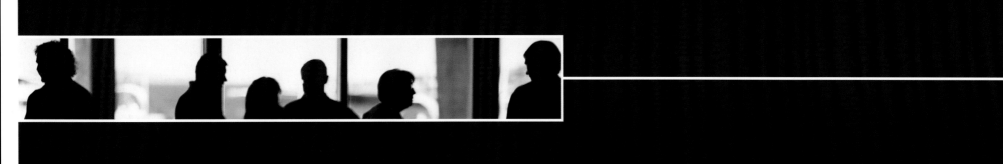

PROFILES OF COMPANIES AND ORGANIZATIONS

Professional, Business, and Consumer Services

International Brotherhood of Electrical Workers Local 343

The hardworking, highly skilled members of this local union chapter keep the Rochester area humming. Their commitment helps maintain good wages and benefits for the brotherhood as well as a reliable, safe power system for the community.

Above: More than 100 members of the International Brotherhood of Electrical Workers (IBEW) Local 343 worked on Mayo Clinic's Gonda Building.

Construction electricians in the Rochester area have been represented by the International Brotherhood of Electrical Workers (IBEW) since 1919, when Local 949, located in Burnsville, Minnesota, was given its charter. Local 949 represented not only construction electricians but also telephone, utility, construction, telecommunications, broadcasting, railroads, government, and manufacturing workers.

In the late 1970s, in an effort to gain a distinct identity for themselves and their work, union construction electricians from the Rochester area and other areas across southern Minnesota petitioned the international union for a separate charter that would better represent its members.

Local Representation

On April 1, 1979, Local 343 won its own charter to represent construction electricians in an area encompassing 26 counties across the southern quarter of Minnesota from the Mississippi River to the South Dakota border. In February 1986, Local 343 and other locals in the state signed the first statewide agreement to represent installers and technicians who install and maintain alarm and security systems, voice and data networks, sound and nurse call systems, and other such systems.

The original local union offices were located in Le Sueur, Minnesota, the geographic center of the local's jurisdiction. Over time, the local concluded that it could better serve members by moving to a location that was chosen not for its geography but for being central to the membership population and to the growth of new construction—and Rochester was the obvious choice. The union offices moved there in 2000, while also maintaining a satellite office in Mankato and apprenticeship training locations in Rochester, Albert Lea, and Mankato.

Today, Local 343 serves more than 1,000 members and 60 signatory contractors within its jurisdiction.

To provide the most qualified and highly trained craftspeople, Local 343 and its contractors provide for members a joint apprenticeship training program as well as continual upgrade training—from first aid and Occupational Safety and Health Administration (OSHA) training to programmable logic controllers and many other subject areas—at no cost. Every year, more than 50 percent of Local 343 members take advantage of these valuable training programs.

Serving the Community

Involvement in the community has always been important to the members of Local 343. They have volunteered their time and skills for numerous worthwhile projects in Rochester and in towns throughout southern Minnesota, working in partnership with charitable organizations such as Ronald McDonald House, the Salvation Army Good Samaritan Dental Clinic, Soldiers Field Veterans Memorial, the Rochester Veterans Memorial at the Rochester Community War Memorial, Boys & Girls Clubs, and Habitat for Humanity, among others.

In 2006 Local 343 completed construction of new offices and a training center that are located just east of Rochester International Airport.

Striving to ensure good wages and benefits, worker safety and security, and opportunities to advance, IBEW Local 343 keeps southern Minnesota wired for success.

Left: Members of IBEW
Local 343 worked as volunteers to install the electrical
wiring for Soldiers Field
Veterans Memorial, which
honors American veterans
of all wars from every
branch of service.

George F. Restovich & Associates, Inc.

Serving the legal needs of the citizens of Rochester and southern Minnesota, this acclaimed general practice law firm, which specializes in civil and criminal trial work, family law, personal injury cases, and estate planning matters, was founded by one of Minnesota's most highly esteemed attorneys.

Since 1993, George F. Restovich & Associates, Inc. has been guided by one of Rochester's most distinguished and accomplished trial attorneys. While George Restovich and his firm handle every type of legal matter, including estate planning, real estate, and contract matters, they specialize in civil and criminal trial practice, including family law and personal injury.

The exclusive *Martindale-Hubbell Bar Register of Preeminent Lawyers* lists George F. Restovich personally, as well as his law firm, as having earned an AV Peer Review Rating. The AV rating is the highest distinction recognized by Martindale-Hubbell and signifies the highest level of legal ability and adherence to the legal professional standards of conduct, ethics, reliability, and diligence.

George F. Restovich received his undergraduate degree in English from the University of Notre Dame in South Bend, Indiana, in 1968, having earned a scholarship to play basketball and baseball for the Irish.

PRACTICE AREAS

- Criminal Defense Law
- Family Law, including Dissolution, Custody, Visitation, and Adoption
- Personal Injury, representing Injured Parties
- Civil Law—Plaintiff and Defendant
- Real Estate Transactions and Litigation
- Estate Planning, including Probate, Wills, Trusts, and Estate Litigation

His legal education began at Louisiana State University Law School in Baton Rouge, where he received his Juris Doctor in 1971. Restovich was admitted to the Louisiana State Bar Association in 1971. In 1973, he was admitted to practice law before the state and federal courts in Minnesota and became a member of the Minnesota State Bar Association. Restovich is admitted to practice before the United States District Court for Minnesota, the United States Court of Appeals for the Eighth Circuit, and the United States Supreme Court.

Restovich's legal career in Rochester began in 1973 when he became an associate attorney in the Patterson Law Office. In 1975, he became a partner in Patterson-Restovich Law Office. He continued to practice law with Patterson-Restovich Law Office until 1993, when he founded George F. Restovich & Associates. Over the years, Restovich has earned a distinguished reputation for hard work and unparalleled success in handling many high-profile civil and criminal cases in Minnesota.

Today, the firm has three associate attorneys—Bruce K. Piotrowski, Anna M. Restovich, and Thomas R. Braun—and three legal assistants.

Restovich also is a member of the Olmsted County Bar Association, the American Bar Association, the Minnesota Trial Lawyers Association, the Association of Trial Lawyers of America, the National Diocesan Attorneys Association, and the American Arbitration Association. He has served as an officer and a member of the board of directors of many nonprofit organizations that serve the Rochester community.

Restovich has been married to Helen J. Restovich since 1968. They are proud of their four children and four grandchildren.

Above: George F. Restovich, one of Minnesota's most successful and distinguished lawyers, has practiced general law in Rochester for some 35 years.

Express Personnel Services

Leaders in the staffing services business for over three decades, Mark and Sheryl Tasler own six franchise offices of one of the largest staffing companies in the country. They specialize in traditional temporary, evaluation hire, core staff placement, professional search, and contract staffing.

In 1974 Mark and Sheryl Tasler, recent college graduates, borrowed $10,000 from a relative to buy a staffing franchise of Acme Personnel in Rochester, pursuing their dream of owning their own business. More than 30 years later, the Midwest natives still call Rochester home. Today, with Norm Doty as their Rochester partner, the couple has employee partners in Winona and Red Wing, Minnesota, and in La Crosse, Eau Claire, and River Falls, Wisconsin. Express Personnel's 600 franchises gross more than $2 billion a year, and the Taslers' six offices consistently rank among the top 10 in the franchise organization. They also take great pride in the numerous production and leadership awards they have earned.

Of their early years, Mark says they had each other, an untapped market, a vision, and a dream. "Other people had a plan B or C for their future, but we decided to put 100 percent of our efforts into our business," he says.

Upon the demise of Acme Personnel in 1980, the Taslers pressed forward with their own staffing firm and in 1985

became the 26th franchise of Express Personnel Services, specializing in traditional temporary help, evaluation hire, core staff placement, and professional search and contract staffing.

Their teams of professionals provide employment opportunities to thousands of people every year, offering staffing solutions to businesses and industry in Rochester and southeast Minnesota. They also own the Express Regional Training Center in Rochester, operated from the same 2518 North Broadway location as Express Personnel Services, and RWJ and Associates,

their professional search and contract staffing division.

Mark is a regional developer for the Express Personnel franchisor, selling franchises in a five-state area and passionately assisting those franchises with their business development.

The Taslers have volunteered their time to many boards and committees, and they support local philanthropic endeavors including the annual Kid's Cup Golf Tournament, which raises funds for children's hospitals. During its 10-year history, the event has raised more than $700,000, with 100 percent of the proceeds going to Mayo Eugenio Litta Children's Hospital in Rochester and Gillette Children's Specialty Healthcare in St. Paul.

Their overall goal, the couple says, is to grow and develop themselves while helping others to do the same. "Rochester is a very giving community with a nucleus of volunteerism," Sheryl says. "We really believe in giving back to the community, which has done so much for us."

Above: Sheryl and Mark Tasler own six top-ranked franchises of Express Personnel Services in Minnesota and Wisconsin.

Rochester Area Chamber of Commerce

By providing its members with unique networking, marketing, and educational opportunities, the Rochester Area Chamber of Commerce and its 250 dedicated volunteers support the Rochester business community, helping to make the city a great place in which to live and do business.

ROCHESTER AREA
CHAMBER OF COMMERCE

Above: Rochester citizens descend on the state capitol each year, part of the Rochester Area Chamber of Commerce's Rochester on Tour at the Capitol event, to advocate their causes with legislators from across the state.

Established to lead, inform, advocate, and advance business interests for its members, the Rochester Area Chamber of Commerce promotes a healthy community and a growing economy. The Rochester Area Chamber of Commerce and its staff provide networking, marketing, and educational opportunities to more than 1,300 member businesses through various committees and task forces. It represents the business community regarding economic and government issues, and it develops programs to help members promote their businesses.

Networking and marketing programs include Business After Hours, the most popular business networking event in Rochester; Business After Hours Extra!, a yearly event where exhibitors display their products and services; the Annual Golf Outing, where members can network and socialize while competing on the golf course; the NewMember Receptions, where members meet one another and also meet the staff of the Rochester Area Chamber of Commerce; and the Annual Member Celebration, when the Rochester Area Chamber of Commerce presents its annual awards to the Volunteer of the Year, the Small Business of the Year, and the Lamp of Knowledge. At this celebration, the incoming chair announces priorities and the new initiative for the upcoming year, followed by entertainment to show appreciation for the chamber's great members.

Publicity and promotional tools include the Rochester Area Chamber of Commerce's monthly newsletter, *Chamber Advantage,* which accepts newsworthy submissions from members about their business; ChamberPak, a low-cost, direct-mail program that reaches 3,900 businesses; event sponsorship, which enables members to support business or social events and increase their organization's visibility; the membership directory, compiled and delivered annually; RelocationPak, which delivers a member's promotional piece to new Rochester residents; ribbon-cutting and ground-breaking ceremonies for new businesses and new locations; and links to member Web sites through the Rochester Area Chamber of Commerce's own site.

The Rochester Area Chamber of Commerce also serves its members by offering valuable educational opportunities. Business Learning Network seminars—conducted by higher-education providers—cover critical topics affecting business owners, such as recruiting and retaining employees in a competitive marketplace. The Educators in the Workplace Institute, a three-day workshop, facilitates partnerships between businesses and education.

Another educational opportunity, the chamber's At Your Service Community Initiative teaches members to understand their customers' needs so they can deliver great service that keeps customers coming back. Customer service affects every organization's bottom line. Quality service helps chamber members to retain customers and to create positive word-of-mouth comments by those customers. The chamber's Leadership Greater Rochester, a comprehensive nine-month program, educates participants about the Rochester community and provides an opportunity to discuss the challenges and issues that face the Rochester area. The program's goals are to identify emerging leaders, to help them expand their community knowledge, and to encourage them to take an active leadership role in the future of Rochester.

The chamber advocates business at all levels of government. Developing and communicating positions on public policy creates value for its members. The chamber provides a forum for the business voice to be heard. As a result, state, local, and federal leaders seek an audience with the members and value member opinions on public policy.

The chamber's Government Affairs program arranges legislative receptions, candidate forums, breakfasts with state legislators, and Rochester on Tour at the Capitol, a day-long event where Rochester citizens go to the state capitol to engage legislators from across the state.

Macken Funeral Home

Delivering quality funeral services to people of all faiths since 1909, this family-owned Rochester business shares a long and proud history with the city. Its dedication to area families, evident since the company's beginning, is still a key element in its business practices.

On the eve of its 100th anniversary, Macken Funeral Home is proud to be the oldest independent, family-owned funeral establishment in Rochester. Founded by Dan Macken in 1909, the business has grown through the years in harmony with the city. It has remained faithful to its founder's philosophy of providing sincere, dedicated service to families of all faiths.

The son of Irish immigrant farmers, Dan Macken was born in nearby Marion Township, Olmsted County, in 1877. He attended the College of St. Thomas in St. Paul and later finished an embalming apprenticeship in the capital city. Upon returning to Rochester, he worked for a funeral establishment before opening his own, which he named the Dan Macken Company. His new funeral establishment at 320 South Broadway also included a furniture business, which was common practice for funeral homes at the time.

In 1920 the furniture operation was discontinued to focus on the funeral business. The firm moved to 220 First Avenue Southwest, the future site of a well-known landmark, China Hall. In 1931 the Dan Macken Company moved to the former Henry Schuster home at 223 Fourth Street Southwest. The business principals at that time were Dan and two of his brothers, Michael and Cyril Macken.

The founder's son, Daniel D. "Dan" Macken Jr., was a student at Loras College in Dubuque, Iowa, when he joined the Army Air Corps, serving three years. He then graduated from the University of Minnesota's Mortuary Science Department in 1950 and subsequently joined his father's firm. In 1962 a new facility was constructed in southeast Rochester at 11th Avenue and Highway 14. By this time Dan Jr. was sole owner and proprietor of the company, renamed Macken Funeral Home.

By 1978 Daniel K. Macken and Timothy J. Macken, sons of Dan Jr., had joined the firm. The brothers had graduated from the University of Minnesota, where they received bachelor's degrees in mortuary science. Daniel K. had served his apprenticeship in St. Paul, and Timothy J. had completed his apprenticeship in Duluth. The two sons worked alongside their father until Dan Jr. retired in 1992.

Today, Daniel K. and Timothy J. Macken, the founder's grandsons, represent the third generation, operating the firm with a qualified staff of licensed morticians and administrative support. Timothy's eldest son, Peter, has joined the firm and represents the fourth generation.

In 1997 a new cremation facility was added to the Macken Funeral Home campus to meet a growing request for alternative services. Macken Funeral Home's main building houses the Colonial Chapel along with visitation and service areas.

In their next century of operations, the Macken family will continue to provide the best of services, facilities, and personnel for the families they serve.

Left: Since 1909, the Macken Funeral Home has faithfully served Rochester. Daniel D. "Dan" Macken Jr. (center) is now retired, and today the company is run by his sons, Daniel K. Macken (left) and Timothy J. Macken (right). The portrait behind them is of founder Dan Macken Sr.

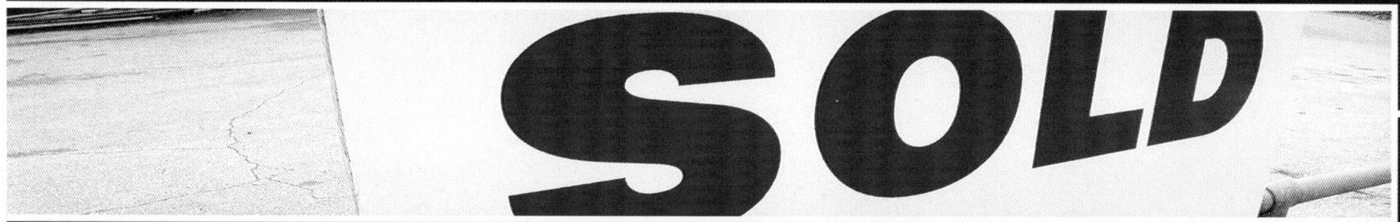
SOLD

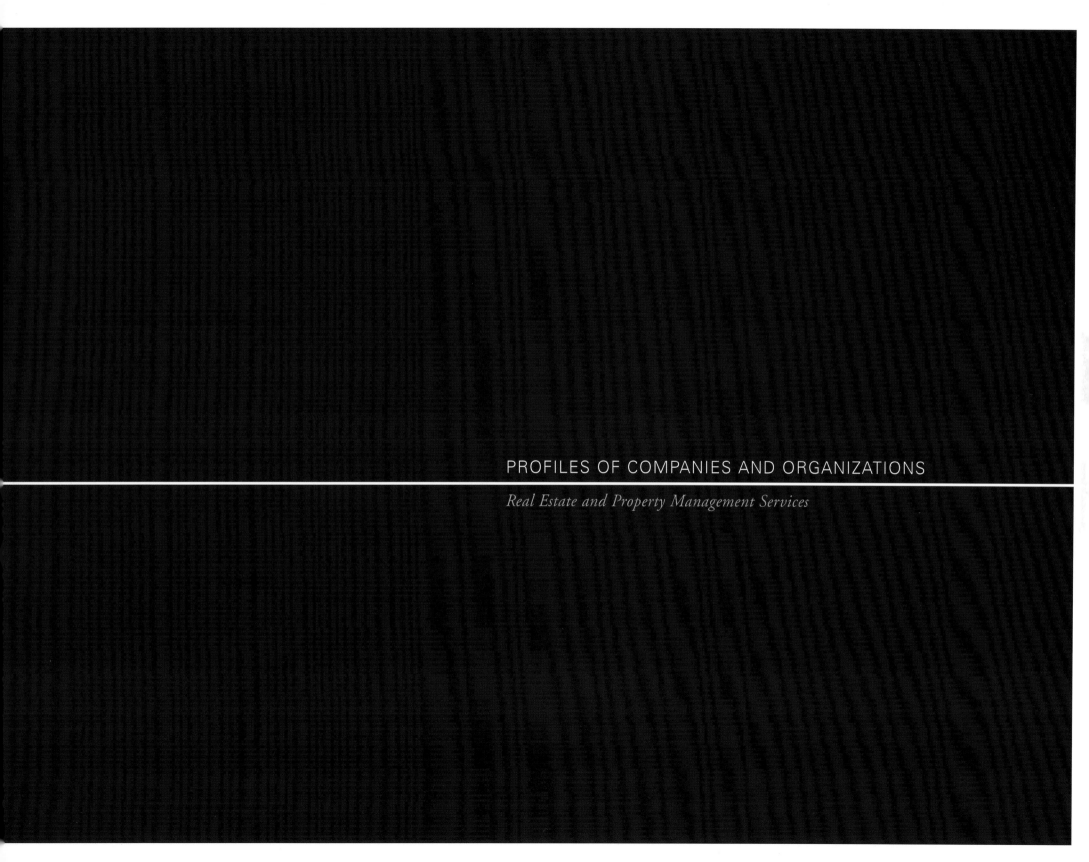

PROFILES OF COMPANIES AND ORGANIZATIONS

Real Estate and Property Management Services

Dominium Management Services

Since 1972, this leading real estate development and management company has served Rochester, the Minneapolis–St.Paul area, and major markets in the upper Midwest, providing superior housing options that ensure maximum value for owners and maximum quality for residents.

A Trusted Business Partner

Dominium Management Services is a privately held real estate company headquartered in Plymouth, Minnesota. Renowned for its many specialties—development and acquisition, financing, management, and marketing—Dominium is a recognized expert in all areas of real estate and has earned a solid reputation as a financially sound development company and accredited management organization. The firm's portfolio includes more than 12,500 units developed and over 16,000 units managed throughout the midwestern and the southeastern United States.

All photos: Dominium Management Services prides itself on offering a wide variety of rental communities that meet any budget, lifestyle, and service expectations.

Dominium consistently surpasses industry standards by developing superior housing options, staffing them with trusted professionals, and striving for peak performance. Clients benefit from the company's excellent reputations with the U.S. Department of Housing and Urban Development (HUD) and local social service agencies. Dominium has also been recognized as an Accredited Management Organization by the Institute of Real Estate Management (IREM).

Dominium has extensive experience with market rate, affordable, subsidized, family, and senior housing and has won numerous design, management, and marketing awards within multifamily trade associations.

Solid working relationships backed by superior performance and innovative ideas are essential in achieving the goals and expectations of property owners and investors. Dominium has been building trusting and financially rewarding partnerships with lenders, vendors, residents, and staff for more than a quarter of a century.

A Trusted Housing Partner

Dominium understands that choosing a place to live is one of the most important choices in life's journey. The right rental choice for anyone must provide a combination of value, comfort, trust, and pride. Dominium is proud to offer a wide variety of rental communities that meet the budgets, lifestyles, and service expectations of all types of renters.

Dominium understands the needs of a first-time renter and appreciates the importance of quality housing for families working toward home owner-ship. Dominium is experienced with

the emotions of selling a home to return to renting, the importance of a perfect fit with senior housing, and even the expectations of someone needing temporary corporate housing.

For more than 35 years, Dominium has been committed to superior resident satisfaction by providing exceptional choices and sound management. Whether the need is for a luxury, senior, traditional, temporary-furnished, pet-friendly, or affordable family rental community, Dominium has it all. The company's number one priority is the satisfaction of its residents.

All photos: Dominium has access to all styles of rental communities, from afford-able family, senior, and traditional communities to pet-friendly and luxury rental communities.

Edina Realty Home Services

A Rochester success story and one of the nation's largest real estate companies, Edina Realty Home Services reinvented the home-buying and home-selling process by providing products and services for every aspect of home ownership. Today, the Edina Realty Rochester office is one of the company's top-ranked branches.

In June 1993, K and K Realty of Rochester, a highly respected, mid-sized company, merged with Edina Realty Home Services, a network of 90 offices and 3,400 sales associates in Minnesota, Wisconsin, and the Dakotas. Edina Realty Rochester has grown to 100 professional, productive REALTORS®; built a new building at 1301 Salem Road, Southwest; and added Edina Realty Mortgage Services and the Edina Realty Title Closing Center.

Edina Realty Rochester and four satellite offices serve the residential and commercial real estate needs, in all price ranges and styles, of all the southeast Minnesota communities, dominating the exceptional properties and new construction markets. Currently, Edina Realty has the greatest number of properties listed in the southeast Minnesota multiple listing service. Edina Realty is a leader in training, technology, and teamwork.

Among southeast Minnesota companies, Edina Realty Rochester is proud to have the highest number of agents who have earned professional designations

through advanced real estate education and documented production. This exemplifies Edina Realty's focus on education, ethics, experience, expertise, and excellence. Honesty, integrity, and commitment have been Edina Realty guidelines since the company was founded in 1955.

Edina Realty understands that buying a home is often the biggest commitment that people make—not only an investment in dollars, but also an investment in family security and comfort. Listing and selling homes are only two of Edina Realty's specialties. The company also offers financing, home owners insurance, moving services, home warranty choices, staging recommendations, marketing consultation, title insurance, and closing services.

Edina Realty attributes its success to finding new and better ways to serve clients, such as expanding services and using the most advanced technology. The company was the first in the Minnesota market to publish detailed property information online, including a listing notification service, online appointment scheduling, a Minnesota open house directory, and a 24-hour interactive hotline system. Edina Realty agents are equipped with innovative mobile phone and personal digital assistant (PDA) software that allows them to access property data from the field.

Edina Realty believes everyone should have a place to call home. In 1996 the company established Edina Realty Foundation to fund organizations that provide housing, food, and clothing to

the homeless and those less fortunate in local communities. Each year Edina Realty Rochester and its satellite offices contribute grants in excess of $20,000 from employee donations and company matching funds to charitable organizations in southeast Minnesota communities. In addition, Edina Realty sales associates and staff participate in a wide variety of community service projects.

Edina Realty Home Services, an affiliate of Home Services of America, one of the largest residential real estate brokerages in the United States, is devoted to providing its sales associates and employees with the technology, training, and work environment to succeed; giving clients unparalleled service; and contributing to the communities it serves.

INH Companies

This Rochester-based real estate firm provides management, maintenance, consulting, accounting, and investment services to individuals and organizations that invest in multifamily and commercial properties. Capable employees and outstanding service ensure that each property performs at the maximum level.

As a full-service real estate firm, INH recognizes that a knowledgeable accounting staff and sophisticated financial software are essential to generating accurate, detailed reports. The company's housing compliance department ensures that government-subsidized apartment communities meet all compliance regulations, and its collections agents address delinquent accounts and unlawful detainer actions.

To best meet client needs, INH employs capable people and gives them the resources they need to provide outstanding service. The company encourages its employees to further their education, join professional industry organizations, and pursue certifications. Multiple employees of INH hold the highly regarded designations of Certified Property Manager (CPM) and Certified Commercial Investment Manager (CCIM).

By keeping each client's goals at the forefront and delivering exceptional service, INH has become one of the largest and most successful real estate firms in Minnesota.

From its offices in Rochester and St. Cloud, Minnesota, INH Companies oversees 6,800 apartment units and 800,000 square feet of commercial property located throughout Minnesota, Iowa, and Nebraska. Founded in 1981 by three Certified Property Managers (CPMs) who wanted to exceed expectations in the area of real estate management, INH also excels in the areas of maintenance and construction, brokerage, and investment-related services for multifamily and commercial real estate. The firm's clients include individuals and institutional property owners.

INH uses a teamwork approach to effectively manage and lease its properties, with each team focused on the client's objectives. More than 80 employees in the company's corporate offices and some 250 who work on-site at the properties all possess the professionalism and expertise to ensure that every property performs at its peak level. A team may comprise a property manager, administrative support, leasing agents, site staff, maintenance technicians, and accounting staff.

Marketing is another INH strength that benefits property owners. The physical aspects of each property are reviewed by multiple team members who combine their efforts to create an aggressive marketing plan. This plan addresses important factors such as amenities, location, vacancy, overall condition, and appearance. Strategies are formed for maximizing tenant retention and market positioning to help make the property a long-term asset.

Both photos: INH Companies provides a full range of property management, maintenance, and financial services throughout Minnesota, Iowa, and Nebraska. Two of INH Companies' Rochester properties are shown here, Woodridge Apartments (left) and the clubhouse interior at Quarry Ridge Apartments (right).

RE/MAX of Rochester was founded in 1981 after two young entrepreneurs, Frank Armstrong and Jim Conway, were introduced to a new concept of real estate by Dave and Gail Liniger, the cofounders of RE/MAX. This concept offered agents maximum compensation, advanced support services, and the freedom they needed to succeed. With enthusiasm and determination, Armstrong and Conway invested in RE/MAX and its vision.

After years of success in the growing Rochester economy, the owners agreed to move RE/MAX of Rochester to the next level of service and hire a managing broker. At the time, RE/MAX of Rochester's platform merged pure RE/MAX ideology with an additional commitment by agents to not compete with one another. In 1995 Duane Sauke became a non-selling managing broker to oversee this covenant, consult on agents' issues, and develop technology. In 2006 Sauke became sole owner of all RE/MAX of Rochester operations.

RE/MAX of Rochester has a successful and dominant presence in the Rochester real estate community. Over the past 15 years, RE/MAX of Rochester has grown from 25 to 50 agents. As a result, RE/MAX of Rochester has led in area market share since 1998. Since 2000, RE/MAX of Rochester has been listed in *Real Trends* magazine each year as a top 500 U.S. brokerage firm. Recently, RE/MAX of Rochester established joint ventures for title and mortgage services to continue the tradition of providing a superior level of informed, professional real estate services to buyers and sellers in Greater Rochester. RE/MAX of Rochester's success rests on the commitment to empower its agents.

RE/MAX of Rochester serves its community through leadership and philanthropy. Its agents have taken leadership roles in real estate associations at both the local and state levels. The company supports four scholarships for the Rochester Community and Technical College (RCTC) Foundation; agencies for senior aid and hunger relief; local music, art, and theater; and Rochester Area Economic Development Inc. (RAEDI). Community involvement allows the company to give back to Rochester for all its support throughout the years.

The future of RE/MAX of Rochester is tied to the development and expansion of the area economy.

Above left: RE/MAX of Rochester's new RE/MAX balloon makes its maiden flight. Above right: With 50 agents, RE/MAX of Rochester has a leading share of the real estate market in the area.

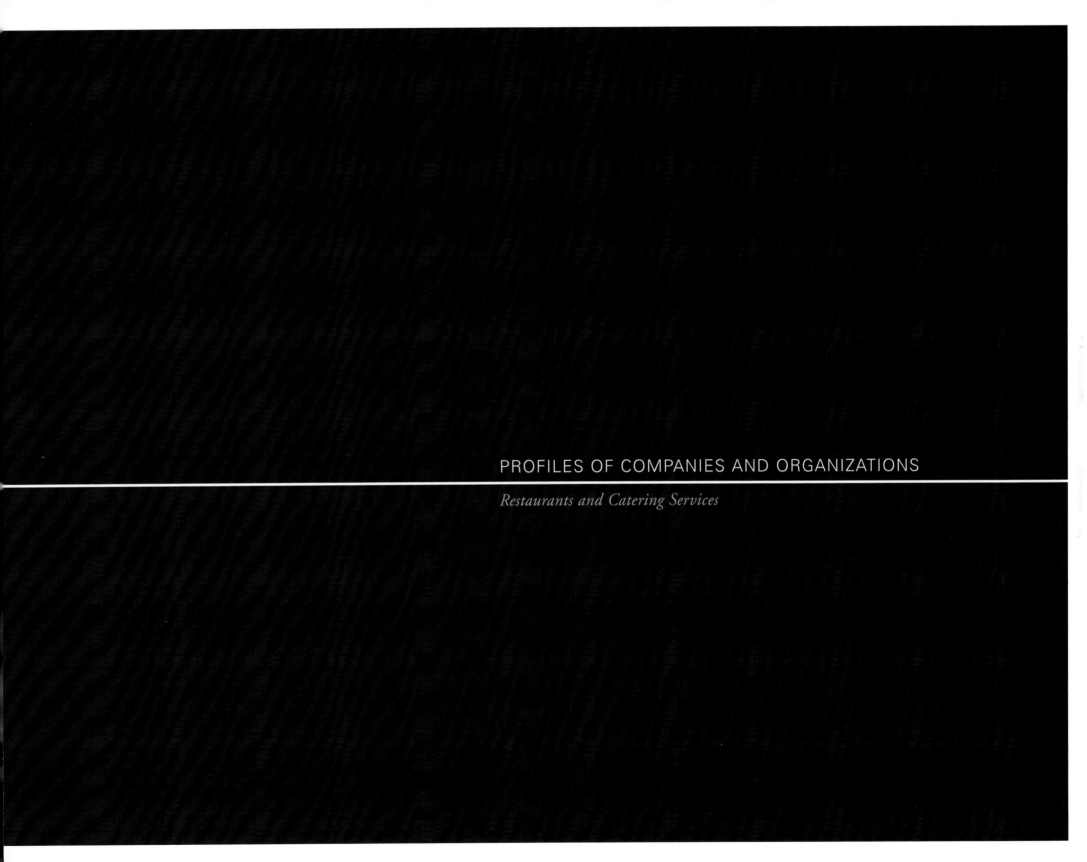

PROFILES OF COMPANIES AND ORGANIZATIONS

Restaurants and Catering Services

Canadian Honker
Restaurant & Catering

For more than two decades, this restaurant and catering business has delighted customers with its delicious homemade foods, excellent service, and welcoming atmosphere. In its catering capacity, it is trusted by thousands of clients—most of whom become repeat clients—to turn every catered party into an event to remember.

In 1984 Joe Powers started a business that would become a fixture of Rochester. The name for the restaurant was inspired by the Canada Goose, which winters in Minnesota. It was a risky proposition: Powers, a 21-year-old entrepreneur, was determined to open his eatery where eight others had failed within a 10-year period, and securing the necessary bank loan was not easy. Powers, however, defied the odds, and today Canadian Honker Restaurant & Catering is a local landmark.

A Restaurant of Success

The first restaurant opened in the front room of a house and could seat 40 people. Business was so good that in 1987 Powers opened a new restaurant, with twice the seating capacity, on the main floor of the Bell Tower Inn, right across the street from Saint Marys Hospital (a Mayo Clinic hospital and one of the largest private hospitals in the world). Business kept growing, and the Canadian Honker Restaurant's popularity soon warranted an even larger space.

In 1998 the company bought land and built a beautiful new restaurant near the previous location. This modern 8,000-square-foot restaurant seats 165 and has outdoor seating, a full bar, and space for live entertainment. Diners find the same delicious homemade food and great service that earned the restaurant its loyal following and outstanding reputation.

The Powers family is a Christian family of Catholic origin; a crucifix hanging in the dining room proudly symbolizes their beliefs.

The Canadian Honker Restaurant serves breakfast, lunch, and dinner, and locals treasure its old-fashioned, fresh-from-scratch food. The number one–selling single item in Rochester is the famous Bunnie's Coconut Cake, according to *Rochester Magazine*. Joe's mother, Bunnie Powers, created this cake, which is sold by the piece or whole. (Demand for whole cakes soars during the holidays.) On weekends, guests can listen to live music and order designer martinis from a full-service bar.

The Caterer to Rochester

The Canadian Honker's catering service, operated by Joe's brother, Cris, offers the same fine food as the restaurant—and much more. Since 1984 the company has catered more than 3,500 weddings and other events for Rochester residents and businesses, guaranteeing 100 percent satisfaction. Canadian Honker Restaurant & Catering provides information about all its services on its Web site (www.canadianhonker.com).

Canadian Honker Catering is southeastern Minnesota's number one caterer. When the U.S. President came to Rochester, the Canadian Honker catered the event. Often, the Canadian Honker caters food for the world-renowned Mayo Clinic as well. The City of Rochester and the governor of Minnesota have also chosen

Canadian Honker Catering for their special events. Customers can expect the highest professionalism in service, food quality, and presentation. Seasonal specials make planning easier for all events, large and small.

Other Establishments of Success

In 1999 the Canadian Honker's outstanding catering reputation led to a concessions contract as in-house caterer for the 120,000-square-foot Mayo Civic Center in Rochester, the largest event facility in southern Minnesota. In 2005 the Powers' company designed and built the Rochester International Event Center next to the Rochester International Airport. This state-of-the-art 25,000-square-foot facility accommodates 850 people for seminars, special events, and weddings. Its large prefunction area and break-out rooms create the appropriate setting for any size group.

Achievements and Awards

Canadian Honker Restaurant & Catering received the Small Business of the Year award in 1988 from the Rochester Chamber of Commerce, as well as state and local awards for volunteerism. Joe Powers cofounded Community Food Response (CFR) in 1993, an organization involving many food vendors over the years. CFR volunteers go to businesses a few times a week and collect all the leftover food to feed the hungry. This is done at a local church. The Powers family donates time, money, and other resources to Habitat for Humanity, the Rochester Area Foundation, Rochesterfest, and other community groups.

Above left: Joe Powers (right) opened his restaurant in 1984. His brother, Cris (left), operates the catering business. Above right: The company designed and built the 25,000-square-foot Rochester International Event Center in 2005.

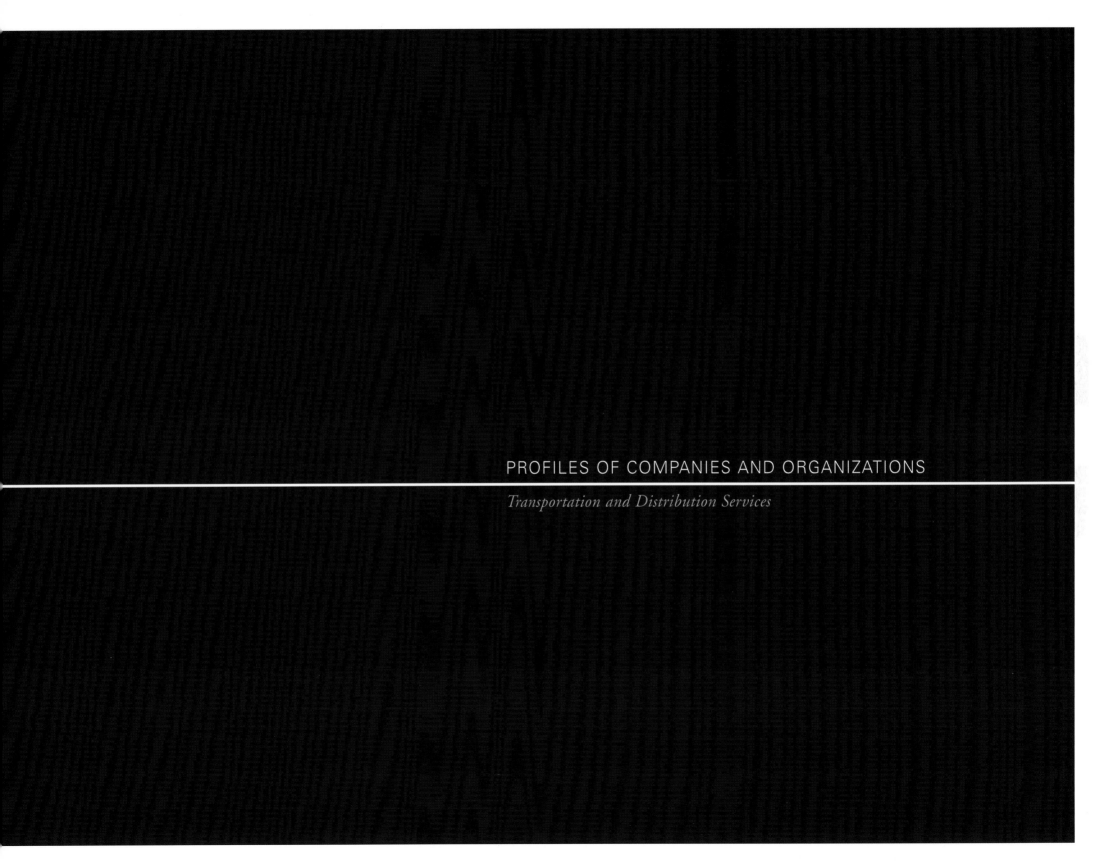

PROFILES OF COMPANIES AND ORGANIZATIONS

Transportation and Distribution Services

Rochester International Airport
Rochester Airport Company

Serving the needs of southeastern Minnesota, as well as parts of Iowa and Wisconsin, this airport provides air service for Mayo Clinic patients as well as travelers throughout the region. The Rochester Airport Company, a wholly owned subsidiary of Mayo Clinic Rochester, operates the airport for the City of Rochester.

Above: Mayo Clinic Rochester operates the city-owned Rochester International Airport through its Rochester Airport Company subsidiary, enabling convenient access to the clinic for patients from around the world. The airport also serves travelers throughout the region.

In 1928 patients at Rochester's Mayo Clinic came and went by train. But doctors and brothers William and Charles Mayo could see that airplanes were the fastest, most convenient way to travel long-distance. At that time, the doctors' vision for an airport in Rochester lacked support from the city, so they took it upon themselves to build an airport by forming the Rochester Airport Company (RAC). The following year, a second airport was opened in southeast Rochester.

The Mayo brothers died within a few months of each other in 1939, but their important work was continued. In 1945 Mayo Clinic deeded the airport land and buildings to the City of Rochester, which then leased them back to RAC. In 1960 the lease ended and was replaced by an airport-operating agreement that made RAC an agent for the city. A dedication of the new Rochester Airport at its present location was held in August 1961.

Not Just for Patients Anymore—Serving the Region and the World

The airport's name was changed to Rochester International Airport in 1995 when U.S. Customs and Border Protection established an office at the airport, enabling international flights. Today the airport's 2,300 acres, its buildings, and most of its equipment are owned by the city. Companies leasing space at the airport include Regent Aviation, DHL Airborne Express, Federal Express, Sleep Inn & Suites, the Hangar Bar & Grill, Home Federal Savings Bank, Take Off Salon, Airport View License Bureau, Pinnacle Engineering, Paramark Property Advisors, and the Rochester International Event Center.

Two major airlines and one minor airline operate out of Rochester International Airport, offering service to travelers throughout the southeastern Minnesota area and parts of Iowa and Wisconsin. American Airlines, Northwest Airlines, and Allegiant Air provide daily and weekly scheduled service to Rochester International Airport. American Airlines offers nonstop jetliner service to and from Rochester from its hub at O'Hare International Airport in Chicago, Illinois, and Northwest Airlines offers daily nonstop jetliner service to and from Rochester from its hubs at Minneapolis–St. Paul International Airport and Detroit Metropolitan Wayne County Airport. Allegiant Air offers the only full-size jet service between Rochester and Las Vegas, Nevada, which benefits the entire midwestern region.

Through owning RAC and operating the airport for the city, Mayo Clinic ensures airport service for patients. This partnership strengthens the Rochester economy while providing Mayo Clinic patients an easy way to get there. The airport is positioned for growth and welcomes new airlines as part of its plan to expand and develop unused land.

Capital improvements at the airport are funded by federal and state money as well as revenues from the airport's operations and fees. RAC is a for-profit corporation and a wholly owned subsidiary of Mayo Clinic Rochester.

Midwest Specialized Transportation, Inc.

Offering specialized transportation services throughout the Midwest and parts of Canada, this Rochester carrier tailors its services to meet customer needs, including oversize loads, consolidated shipments, contract carriage, special equipment, and scheduled pickups and deliveries.

Midwest Specialized Transportation, Inc. dependably hauls specialized cargo from the Midwest to all points in the continental United States and to six Canadian provinces. Founded in 1967, the company credits a "can-do" philosophy for its steady growth and long list of satisfied customers. Its consistently high service, experienced and qualified personnel, outstanding safety records, and well-maintained late-model tractors also factor into its success.

Midwest's goal—do the best possible job for every customer—goes hand in hand with its business strategy: anticipate customer needs and adapt to meet them. The company has an array of equipment for moving almost any cargo, from construction equipment to cryogenic tanks to time-sensitive printed materials. Tractors with satellite equipment allow the home office in Rochester to monitor shipments, and constant weather tracking enables drivers to choose the best route to their destinations.

Tailored services are part of the company's commitment to customer satisfaction. For instance, Midwest can consolidate shipments to cut freight costs. Its fleet can make an unrestricted number of stops during transit to load or unload. To expedite delivery, Midwest brings in two drivers when time is scarce. Job site pickups and deliveries are also a Midwest specialty, and the company has a nationwide reputation for expertise and experience in hauling oversize loads that require special trailers in the company's fleet.

Midwest employees enjoy flexibility and a raft of benefits. Drivers can choose from dedicated runs, time-sensitive van operations throughout the nation, or machinery runs throughout the Midwest. The company provides late-model air-ride equipment with advanced communication systems, programs that reward driver safety and recognize length of service to the company, a 401(k) benefits package with company contribution, amenities for driver comfort and convenience on the road, and medical, dental, life, and disability insurance.

Comprehensive service, specialized equipment, and exemplary safety achievements make Midwest one of the leading carriers in the business, and a company where opportunities abound.

Above: Midwest Specialized Transportation, Inc., in Rochester, Minnesota, is committed to providing professional and quality transportation services to meet each customer's specialized trucking needs.

Rochester Cartage, Inc.

This trucking company, which puts safety and service before everything else, transports food products and general commodities throughout the Midwest and across the United States from its headquarters in Rochester. Since 1986 it has succeeded as an industry and community leader.

Rochester Cartage, Inc. began hauling commodities across the country in 1986, with one driver and one truck. Today, the company's 23 drivers, 22 trucks, and 31 trailers ship food products and general commodity freight through the Midwest and parts of the eastern and southeastern United States. This contract carrier's clients include Seneca Foods, the Rochester Meat Company, Kemps, Rochester Cheese Sales, and Gauthier Industries.

Rochester Cartage puts safety and service above all else. First, it employs safe, conscientious, professional drivers who know the nation's highways backward and forward; second, it strives to ensure the safety, personal health, and industry achievement of its entire staff; and third, it requires all personnel to be Highway Watch–trained. Highway Watch is a national program administered in Minnesota by the Minnesota Trucking Association (MTA), funded by the American Trucking Associations (ATA), and carried out in cooperation with the Department of Homeland Security in order to maintain highway safety and security.

For its outstanding safety record, Rochester Cartage has won a string of safety awards, including the 2003, 2004, 2005, and 2006 Governor's Outstanding Achievement Award for excellence in preventing occupational injuries; six first-place safety awards from the MTA; and three National Fleet Safety awards from the Truckload Carriers Association (winning first place in 2004, second place in 2006, and third place in 2003). In addition, Rochester Cartage garnered an Award of Excellence for safety in 2003 from its insurance carrier, Continental Western Group of Des Moines, Iowa, as well as a letter of commendation in 2004 for achievement in safety from its insurance agency, Hatch Agency, Inc., of Minnetonka, Minnesota.

Rochester Cartage's president and owner, Doug Coen, has been an MTA board member since 1994 and has served on the MTA's executive board since 2003. Coen was also elected to serve as the MTA's chairman from 2006 through 2007. He was named Safety Director of the Year by the MTA in 1996 and received the MTA's Presidents Award in 2000. Coen earned the Presidents Award by demonstrating

leadership in establishing meaningful relationships with the trucking industry.

In the Rochester community, Rochester Cartage supports the Rochester Area Family YMCA. It also participates in fund-raisers and walkathons that benefit efforts to cure cancer, diabetes, multiple

sclerosis, and muscular dystrophy. The company's involvement with the MTA includes sponsoring its annual conference and scholarship program and serving as a drop-off site for the annual MTA Trucks & Toys campaign, which collects toys for hundreds of needy children.

Cherbo Publishing Group

Cherbo Publishing Group's business-focused, art book–quality publications, which celebrate the vital spirit of enterprise, are custom books that are used as high-impact economic development tools to enhance reputations, increase profits, and provide global exposure for businesses and organizations.

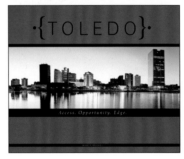

About CPG Publications

CPG has created books for some of America's leading organizations, including the U.S. Chamber of Commerce, Empire State Development, California Sesquicentennial Foundation, Chicago O'Hare International Airport, and the Indiana Manufacturers Association. Participants have included ConAgra, Dow Chemical Company, Lucent Technologies, Merck & Company, and BlueCross/BlueShield.

CPG series range from history books to economic development/relocation books and from business reports to publications of special interest. The economic development series spotlights the outstanding economic and quality-of-life advantages of fast-growing cities, counties, regions, or states. The annual business reports provide an economic snapshot of individual cities, regions, or states. The commemorative series marks milestones for corporations, organizations, and professional and trade associations.

To find out how CPG can help you celebrate a special occasion, or for information on how to showcase your company or organization, contact Jack Cherbo at 818-783-0040, extension 26, or visit www.cherbopub.com.

Both pages, all: Cherbo Publishing Group produces custom books for historical, professional, and government organizations. These fine publications promote the economic development of America's cities, regions, and states by chronicling their history—the people, enterprises, industries, and organizations that have made them great.

Jack Cherbo, Cherbo Publishing Group president and CEO, has been breaking new ground in the sponsored publishing business for more than 40 years.

"Previously, the cost of creating a handsome book for business developments or commemorative occasions fell directly on the sponsoring organization," Cherbo says. "My company pioneered an entirely new concept—funding these books through the sale of corporate profiles."

Cherbo honed his leading edge in Chicago, where he owned a top advertising agency before moving into publishing. Armed with a degree in business administration from Northwestern University, a mind that never stopped, and a keen sense of humor, Cherbo set out to succeed— and continues to do just that.

Cherbo Publishing Group (CPG), formerly a wholly owned subsidiary of

Jostens, Inc., a Fortune 500 company, has been a privately held corporation since 1993. CPG is North America's leading publisher of quality custom books for commercial, civic, historical, and trade associations. Publications range from hardcover state, regional, and commemorative books to softcover state and regional business reports. The company is headquartered in Encino, California, and operates regional offices in Philadelphia, Minneapolis, and Houston.

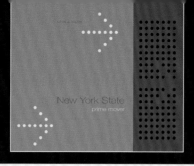

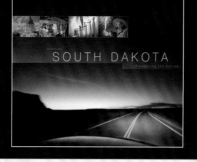

Select CPG Publications

VISIONS OF OPPORTUNITY
City, Regional, and State Series

ALABAMA *The Progress, The Promise*

AMERICA & THE SPIRIT OF ENTERPRISE
Century of Progress, Future of Promise

CALIFORNIA *Golden Past, Shining Future*

CONNECTICUT *Chartered for Progress*

DELAWARE *Incorporating Vision in Industry*

EVANSVILLE *At the Heart of Success*

FORT WORTH *Where the Best Begins*

GREATER PHOENIX
Expanding Horizons

INDIANA
Crossroads of Industry and Innovation

JACKSONVILLE
Where the Future Leads

LUBBOCK, TEXAS
Gem of the South Plains

NASHVILLE *Amplified*

MICHIGAN *America's Pacesetter*

MILWAUKEE *Midwestern Metropolis*

MISSOURI *Gateway to Enterprise*

NEW YORK STATE *Prime Mover*

NORTH CAROLINA *The State of Minds*

OKLAHOMA *The Center of It All*

SOUTH DAKOTA *Pioneering the Future*

TOLEDO *Access. Opportunity. Edge.*

UPSTATE NEW YORK
Corridor to Progress

WESTCHESTER COUNTY, NEW YORK
Headquarters to the World

WEST VIRGINIA *Reaching New Heights*

LEGACY
Commemorative Series

ALBERTA AT 100
Celebrating the Legacy

**BUILD IT & THE CROWDS
WILL COME**
Seventy-Five Years of Public Assembly

CELEBRATE SAINT PAUL
150 Years of History

DAYTON *On the Wings of Progress*

THE EXHIBITION INDUSTRY
The Power of Commerce

IDAHO *The Heroic Journey*

MINNEAPOLIS *Currents of Change*

**NEW YORK STATE ASSOCIATION
OF FIRE CHIEFS**
Sizing Up a Century of Service

VISIONS TAKING SHAPE
*Celebrating 50 Years of the Precast/
Prestressed Concrete Industry*

ANNUAL BUSINESS REPORTS
MINNESOTA REPORT *2007*

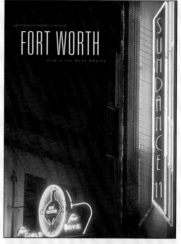
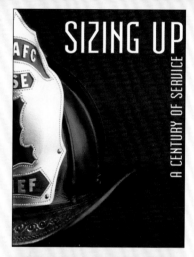
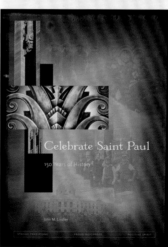
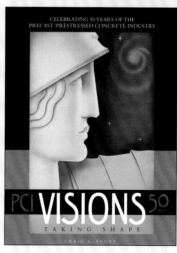
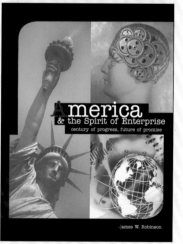

SELECTED BIBLIOGRAPHY

Alperovitz, Gar. "Medicine With a Heart." *Technology Review*, April 1993. http://mayoclinic.org/about/techreview.html (accessed May 22, 2007).

Anderson, Gary Clayton. *Kinsmen of Another Kind: Dakota-White Relations in the Upper Mississippi Valley, 1650–1862*. Rev. ed. St. Paul: Minnesota Historical Society Press, 1997.

Andreas, A. T. *An Illustrated Historical Atlas of the State of Minnesota*. Chicago: Andreas, 1874.

Anifson, Scott Fleming. "The Prehistory of the Prairie Lake Region in the Northeastern Plains." Ph.D. diss., University of Minnesota, 1987.

Bauer, Roy, Emilio Collar, and Victor Tang. *The Silverlake Project: Transformation at IBM*. New York: Oxford University Press, 1992.

Bordner, Kenneth L. "Rochester Study Report, Rochester, Minnesota." Consultant's report, 1972.

Bordner Consultants. "Northgate Shopping Center, Rochester, Minn." 1977.

Boyett, Joseph H., Stephen Schwartz, Laurence Osterwise, and Roy Bauer. *The Quality Journey: How Winning the Baldrige Sparked the Remaking of IBM*. New York: Dutton, 1993.

Carroll, Paul. *Big Blues: The Unmaking of IBM*. New York: Crown, 1993.

City of Rochester, Minnesota. "Economic Characteristics." http://www.rochestermn.gov/business/economiccharacteristics.asp (accessed May 22, 2007).

Clapesattle, Helen. *The Doctors Mayo*. New ed. Rochester, MN: Mayo Foundation for Medical Education and Research, 1990. First published 1941 by University of Minnesota Press.

Crenlo. "History." http://www.crenlo.com/history.html (accessed May 22, 2007).

Cronon, William. *Nature's Metropolis*. New York: W. W. Norton, 1991.

DeVol, Ross, and Perry Wong. "America's High-Tech Economy: Growth, Development and Risks for Metropolitan Areas." *Milken Institute Research Report*, July 13, 1999. http://www.milkeninstitute.org/publications/publications.taf?function=detail&ID=15&cat=ResRep (accessed July 20, 2007).

Diedrich, Mark F. *Famous Chiefs of the Eastern Sioux*. Minneapolis: Coyote Books, 1987.

———. *The Chiefs Wapahasha*. Rochester, MN: Coyote Books, 2004.

Dixon, George. "Clinical Detachment: The Mayo Has Outgrown Rochester." *Corporate Report Minnesota* (April 1988): 33–40.

Donovan, Frank P., Jr. "The Amazing Great Western." *Railroad Magazine* 61, no. 4 (September 1953): 12–32.

Douglas, Robert. "A Clinic City on Minnesota's Prairie." *New York Times Magazine*, October 21, 1928.

Fletcher, Merna Irene. "Rochester: A Professional Town." *Economic Geography* 23, no. 2 (April 1947): 143–51.

Folwell, William Watts. *A History of Minnesota: Volume III*. Rev. ed. St. Paul: Minnesota Historical Society, 1969.

Frame, Robert M. *Millers to the World: Minnesota's Nineteenth Century Water Power Flour Mills*. St. Paul: Minnesota Historical Society, 1977.

———. Research files on flour mills. Minnesota Historical Society, St. Paul.

Garr, Doug. *IBM Redux: Lou Gerstner & The Business Turnaround of the Decade*. New York: HarperBusiness, 1999.

Greenhouse, Linda. *Becoming Justice Blackmun: Harry Blackmun's Supreme Court Journey*. New York: Henry Holt & Co., 2005.

Grimsrud, George. "The Mayo Clinic." *Wall Street Journal*, January 31, 1969.

Hartzell, Judith. *I Started All This: The Life of Dr. William Worrall Mayo.* Greenville, SC: Arvi Books, 2004.

Hill, W. H., ed. *History of Olmsted County, Minnesota.* Chicago: H. H. Hill & Company, 1883.

Hodgson, Harriet W. *Rochester: City of the Prairie.* Northridge, CA: Windsor Publications, 1989.

Hughes, Thomas. *Indian Chiefs of Southern Minnesota.* Mankato, MN: Free Press, 1927.

Johnson, Frederick L. *Goodhue County, Minnesota: A Narrative History.* Red Wing, MN: Goodhue County Historical Society Press, 2000.

Johnson, Hildegard Binder. *Order Upon the Land: The U.S. Rectangular Land Survey and the Upper Mississippi Country.* New York: Oxford University Press, 1976.

Kahler Corporation. "60 Years of Caring . . . The Kahler Corporation 1917–1977." n.d.

Lass, William E. *Minnesota: A History.* 2nd ed. New York: W. W. Norton, 1998.

Lehmberg, Stanford, and Ann M. Pflaum. *The University of Minnesota 1945–2000.* Minneapolis: University of Minnesota Press, 2001.

Luecke, John C. *The Chicago and Northwestern in Minnesota.* Eagan, MN: Grenadier Publications, 1990.

Marschner, Francis J. *The Original Vegetation of Minnesota, Compiled from U.S. General Land Office Survey Notes by Francis J. Marschner.* With notes by Miron Heinselman. St. Paul: North Central Forest Experiment Station, 1974.

Mayall, Samuel. *Report of the Proceedings of the Anti-Monopoly Convention Held at Rochester, Minn., Dec. 1st, 1870.* Rochester, MN: Federal Union, 1870.

Mayo Clinic. "About Discovery's Edge." http://discoverysedge.mayo.edu/about_us.cfm (accessed May 22, 2007).

———. "Bone: What Builds It Up, Breaks It Down and Makes It Break?" *Discovery's Edge.* http://discoverysedge.mayo.edu/brittle_bones/ (accessed May 22, 2007).

———. "The Rochester Carillon." 2006.

Mayo Clinic College of Medicine–Mayo Graduate School. "History." http://www.mayo.edu/mgs/history.html (accessed May 22, 2007).

Mayo Clinic College of Medicine–Mayo School of Continuing Medical Education. "Dean's Message." http://www.mayo.edu/cme/deans-message.html (accessed May 22, 2007).

Mayo Clinic College of Medicine–Mayo School of Health Sciences. "MSHS History." http://www.mayo.edu/mshs/history.html (accessed May 22, 2007).

McCracken, Ken. "Clinic Taking First Crack at Advertising." *Rochester Post-Bulletin,* February 9, 1985.

Meinig, D. W. *Continental America, 1800–1867.* New Haven: Yale University Press, 1993.

Miller, George H. *Railroads and the Granger Laws.* Madison, WI: University of Wisconsin Press, 1971.

Minnesota Partnership for Biotechnology and Medical Genomics. " Minnesota Partnership Celebrates Construction of New Research Facility." http://www.minnesotapartnership.info/pressreleases/2005-0809/ (accessed May 22, 2007).

Minnesota Territory. Petitions (1857) to Legislative Assembly. Minnesota Historical Society. Box 115.I.19.12F.

Mitchell, W. H. *History of the County of Olmsted.* Rochester: Shaver & Eaton, 1866.

SELECTED BIBLIOGRAPHY

Norberg, Arthur, and Jeffrey Yost. *IBM Rochester: A Half Century of Innovation.* Rochester, MN: IBM Rochester, 2006.

Ohsann, Tim. "Rochester Wins Coveted Honor." *Think*, no. 6 (1990): 16–20.

Ojakangas, Richard W., and Charles L. Matsch. *Minnesota's Geology.* Minneapolis: University of Minnesota Press, 1982.

Onuf, Peter S. *Statehood and Union: A History of the Northwest Ordinance.* Bloomington, IN: Indiana University Press, 1987.

Opheim, Teresa. "Justice Harry A. Blackmun." *The Mayo Alumnus*, 1990.

Parker, Walter. "Can It Keep Up the Pace?" *St. Paul Pioneer Press*, January 11, 1993.

Phillips, James L., and James A. Brown, eds. *Archaic Hunters and Gatherers in the American Midwest.* New York: Academic Press, 1983.

Poch, George A. *Soil Survey of Olmsted County, Minnesota.* Washington, D.C.: Soil Conservation Service of U.S. Department of Agriculture, 1980.

Prosser, Richard S. *Rails to the North Star: One Hundred Years of Railroad Evolution in Minnesota.* Minneapolis: Dillon Press, 1966.

Pugh, Emerson W. *Building IBM: Shaping an Industry and Its Technology.* Cambridge, MA: MIT Press, 1995.

Roberts, Paul. "The Agenda—Total Teamwork." *Fast Company*, March 1999. http://www.fastcompany.com/online/23/totteam.html (accessed May 22, 2007).

Rochester Area Economic Development. "About Rochester: Community, Economy, Major Employers." http://www.raedi.org/economic_overview.html (accessed May 22, 2007).

———. "Rochester Minnesota Helps Drive Development of Bioscience Industry." http://www.raedi.org/bioscience.html (accessed May 22, 2007).

Rochester Community and Technical College. "Rochester Community and Technical College 1915 to 2005." 2005.

Rochester Convention and Visitors Bureau. "Attractions." http://www.rochestercvb.org/visitors/thingstodo.asp?subcat=Attractions (accessed May 22, 2007).

———. "Dining Guide." http://www.rochestercvb.org/visitors/dining.asp (accessed May 22, 2007).

Rochester Free Press, "A Tour Among the Business Houses at Rochester," March 24, 1858.

Rochester International Airport. "Airlines & Shipping." http://www.rochesterintlairport.com/airline-shipping.php (accessed May 22, 2007).

Rochester, Minn. New York: Sanborn Map and Publishing Company, 1884, 1890.

Rochester Post, "The Anti-Railroad Convention," December 3, 1870.

Rochester Post-Bulletin. Celebrating 150 Years, Rochester & Olmsted County. Vancouver, WA: Pediment Publishing, 2003.

———, "Mayo Clinic," March 22, 1997.

Rochester Public Library. "Early History of the Library." n.d.

Sanford, Dr. A. H. "The Dubuque Trail." Manuscript. Minnesota Historical Society. n.d.

Sansome, Constance Jefferson. *Minnesota Underfoot: A Field Guide to the State's Outstanding Geologic Features.* Stillwater, MN: Voyageur Press, 1983.

Schwartz, George M., and George A. Thiel. *Minnesota's Rocks and Waters: A Geological Story.* Rev. ed. Minneapolis: University of Minnesota Press, 1963.

Sinclair, D. "Inland Towns." *Winona Republican*, May 13, 1856.

———. "Olmsted County." *Winona Republican*, September 2, 1856.

Sterling, David N. "Photographs to Phonographs: The Conley Story." *The Photographic Collectors' Newsletter* 3, no. 4 (1975): 4–17.

St. Mane, Ted. *Images of America: Rochester, Minnesota*. Charleston, SC: Arcadia Publishing, 2003.

St. Paul Advertiser, "Rochester, Olmstead [*sic*] Co.," December 13, 1856.

The Rochester Centennial, 1854–1954. Rochester, MN: Rochester Centennial Association, 1954.

Theler, James L., and Robert F. Boszhardt. *Twelve Millennia: Archaeology of the Upper Mississippi River Valley*. Iowa City: University of Iowa Press, 2003.

Ulland, Dick. "Happy Anniversary IBM Rochester." *IBM Rochester News*, October 1991.

United States Census Bureau. *Census of Manufacturing*. Washington, D.C., 1860, 1870, 1880.

University Center Rochester. "University Center Rochester—A Spectrum of Learning–UCR Campus." http://www.roch.edu/html-spectrum/ucr_campus .html (accessed May 22, 2007).

University of Minnesota. "University of Minnesota Announces Enhancements in Rochester." Press release, November 16, 2006. http://www1.umn.edu/ umnnews (accessed May 22, 2007).

University of Minnesota Morris–Center for Small Towns. "Census Data for Rochester City." http://www.mrs.umn.edu/services/cst/index.htm (accessed May 22, 2007).

University of Minnesota Rochester. "About UMR." http://www.r.umn.edu/ 01_about.htm (accessed May 22, 2007).

Upham, Warren. *Minnesota Geographic Names: Their Origin and Historic*

Significance. Rev. ed. St. Paul: Minnesota Historical Society, 1969.

U.S. Surveyor General. Notes for Township 107 North, Range 14 West, and for Township 106 North, Range 14 West. Minnesota Historical Society. Box 111.E.6.5(B). Also, surveyors' annotated maps on microfiche.

Waters, Thomas F. *The Streams and Rivers of Minnesota*. Minneapolis: University of Minnesota Press, 1977.

Willson, Charles C. "The Successive Chiefs Named Wabasha." In *Minnesota Historical Society Collections, Vol. XII*. St. Paul: Minnesota Historical Society, 1908.

Winchell, Newton H. *The Geology of Minnesota: Vol. VI of the Final Report: Geological Atlas with Synoptical Descriptions*. St. Paul: Pioneer Press Company, 1901.

Winona Republican, "On the Wing," April 28, 1857.

Winona State University Rochester Center. "About WSU Rochester." http://winona.edu/rochester/aboutwsurochester.html (accessed May 22, 2007).

Wolfe, Carol. "Our Rochester—Then and Now." In *Rochester Diamond Jubilee, 1854–1929: June 9–12, 1929*. 1929.

Woods, Thomas A. *Knights of the Plow: Oliver H. Kelley and the Origins of the Grange in Republican Ideology*. Ames, IA: Iowa State University Press, 1991.

Woolworth, Alan. Papers. Minnesota Historical Society.

———, and Nancy L. Woolworth. "Eastern Dakota Settlement and Subsistence Patterns Prior to 1851." *Minnesota Archaeologist* 39, no. 2 (1980): 71–89.

PHOTO CREDITS

Unless otherwise noted, all images that appear on the same page are listed from left to right.

PHOTO CREDITS

Unless otherwise noted, all images that appear on the same page are listed from left to right.

Page 30, bottom left: Courtesy, Olmsted County Historical Society

Page 31: Courtesy, Olmsted County Historical Society

Page 32, 33: Courtesy, Olmsted County Historical Society

Page 34: Courtesy, Olmsted County Historical Society

Page 35, left: Courtesy, Olmsted County Historical Society

Page 35, right: Courtesy, Olmsted County Historical Society

Page 36, top left: Courtesy, Minnesota Historical Society

Page 36, right: Courtesy, Minnesota Historical Society

Page 36, bottom left: Courtesy, Minnesota Historical Society

Page 37: Courtesy, Minnesota Historical Society

Page 38, top: Courtesy, Olmsted County Historical Society

Page 38, bottom: Courtesy, Mayo Clinic

Page 39: Courtesy, Olmsted County Historical Society

Page 40, left: Courtesy, Olmsted County Historical Society

Page 40, right: Courtesy, Olmsted County Historical Society

Page 41, left: Courtesy, Olmsted County Historical Society

Page 41, right: Courtesy, Olmsted County Historical Society

Page 42, top: Courtesy, Olmsted County Historical Society

Page 42, bottom: Courtesy, Minnesota Historical Society

Page 43: Courtesy, Minnesota Historical Society

Page 44, 45: Courtesy, Olmsted County Historical Society

Page 46: © Time & Life Pictures/Getty Images

Page 47, top: Courtesy, Minnesota Historical Society

Page 47, bottom: © Corbis

Page 48, top: © Bettman/Corbis

Page 48, bottom: © Bettman/ Corbis

Page 49: Courtesy, IBM

Page 50, top: Courtesy, Minnesota Historical Society

Page 50, bottom: Courtesy, IBM

Page 51: Courtesy, IBM

Page 52: Courtesy, Rochester Post-Bulletin

PATRONS

Ameriprise Financial, Inc.*

Apollo Dental Center*

Armon Architecture

Benchmark Electronics, Inc./

    Pemstar Inc.*

Bigelow Homes*

Canadian Honker Restaurant

    & Catering*

Chafoulias Companies*

Charter Communications*

City of Rochester*

C. O. Brown Agency, Inc.*

Dominium Management

    Services*

Edina Realty Home Services*

Ellerbe Becket, Inc.*

Express Personnel Services*

Foldcraft Co.*

Franciscan Sisters of Rochester,

    The*

Gauthier Industries Inc.*

George F. Restovich &

    Associates, Inc.*

Hammel, Green and

    Abrahamson, Inc.*

Herbergers, Inc.

Hexum Companies, The*

HiMEC Mechanical, Inc.

IBM Rochester*

Ideacom Mid-America*

INH Companies*

International Brotherhood of

    Electrical Workers Local 343*

JLC Food Systems, Inc.

Johnson Controls, Inc.*

Kahler Hotels*

Knutson Construction Services*

Lourdes High School

Macken Funeral Home*

Mayo Clinic*

McGhie & Betts, Inc.*

McNeilus Corporation*

Merrill Lynch & Co., Inc.*

Midwest Specialized

    Transportation, Inc.*

Olmsted Medical Center*

* For additional information about these companies and organizations, please refer to the index on page xi

Pace Dairy Foods*

Palmer Soderberg

Pharmaceutical Specialties,
    Inc.*

Precision Chiropractic Center*

Professional Instruments
    Company, Inc.

Prosthetic Laboratories of
    Rochester, Inc.*

RE/MAX of Rochester*

R. Fleming Construction, Inc.

Rochester Area Chamber
    of Commerce*

Rochester Area Foundation*

Rochester Athletic Club*

Rochester Cartage, Inc.*

Rochester Civic Theatre*

Rochester Community and
    Technical College*

Rochester International
    Airport—Rochester
    Airport Company*

Rochester Public Schools*

Rochester Public Utilities*

Rochester Sand & Gravel

Rochester Swim Club Orcas*

Saint Mary's University of
    Minnesota—Schools of
    Graduate and Professional
    Programs–Rochester Center*

Samaritan Bethany Inc.*

Sargent's Landscape Nursery,
    Inc.

Southeastern Minnesota Oral
    and Maxillofacial Surgery
    Associates*

Summit Custom Homes*

TSP*

University of Minnesota
    Rochester*

Weis Builders, Inc.*

Winona State University*

Woodruff Company*

Yaggy Colby Associates*

Ye Olde Butcher Shoppe
    of Rochester

cherbo publishing group, inc.

TYPOGRAPHY

Principal faces used: Adobe Garamond, designed by Robert Slimbach in 1989,
which was derived from previous designs by Claude Garamond, Jean Jannon, and
Robert Granjon; Univers, designed by Adrian Frutiger in 1957; Helvetica, designed
by Matthew Carter, Edouard Hoffmann, and Max Miedinger in 1959.

HARDWARE

Macintosh G5 desktops, digital color laser printing with Xerox Docucolor 250, digital
imaging with Creo EverSmart Supreme

SOFTWARE

QuarkXPress, Adobe Illustrator, Adobe Creative Suite CS2, Adobe Acrobat,
Microsoft Word, Eye-One Pro by Gretagmacbeth, Creo Oxygen, FlightCheck

PAPER

Text Paper: #80 Luna Matte

Bound in Rainbow® recycled content papers from
Ecological Fibers, Inc.

Dust Jacket: #100 Sterling-Litho Gloss